LEADING THE WAY:

Student Engagement and Nationally Competitive Awards

THE NATIONAL ASSOCIATION OF FELLOWSHIPS ADVISORS

Edited by Suzanne McCray

THE UNIVERSITY OF ARKANSAS PRESS

FAYETTEVILLE

2009

ISBN-10: 1-55728-920-4
ISBN-13: 978-1-55728-920-9

13 12 11 10 09 5 4 3 2 1

Designer: Ellen Beeler
Composition: Publication Services, Inc.

∞The paper used in this publication meets the minimum requirements of the American
National Standard for Permanence of Paper for Printed Library Materials Z39.48-1984.

Library of Congress Cataloging-in-Publication Data

National Association of Fellowships Advisors. Conference (4th : 2007 : Washington,
D.C.) Leading the way : student engagement and nationally competitive awards /
edited by Suzanne McCray.
        p. cm.
  Includes bibliographical references and index.
  ISBN 978-1-55728-920-9 (pbk. : alk. paper)
1. Scholarships—United States—Evaluation—Congresses. 2. College students—
Scholarships, fellowships, etc.—United States—Congresses. I. McCray, Suzanne, 1956-
II. National Association of Fellowships Advisors. III. Title.
  LB2338.N22 2007
  378.3'40973—dc22
                                2009022900

Contents

Acknowledgments   *v*

Introduction   *ix*
  SUZANNE MCCRAY

1 State Department Initiatives for International Academic Exchange
  MARIANNE CRAVEN   *1*

2 Non Ducor, Duco
  Leadership and the Truman Scholarship Application
  TARA YGLESIAS   *9*

3 How Soon Is Too Soon?
  Identifying Qualified Applicants
  PATTI ROSS, VANESSA EVANS,
  MIKE MALLORY, AND COLLEEN QUINT   *19*

4 The National Institutes of Health/Oxford/Cambridge Scholars Program
  A New Approach to Biomedical PhD Training
  MICHAEL J. LENARDO   *33*

5 Understanding the Odds
  A Reader's Perspective
  DOUG CUTCHINS   *43*

6 Creating Opportunities for Experiential Education in a Resource-Strained Environment
  PAULA WARRICK   *51*

7   A Newcomer's Guide to Scholarship Advising
CAROL SHINER WILSON   *59*

8   Encouraged to Apply
Diversity and the Scholarship Process
LISA J. KNEPSHIELD   *67*

9   Preparing for *the* Interview
Advice from a Gates Cambridge Scholar and Fellowships Advisor
LANCE OWEN   *75*

10   Involving Faculty in the Scholarship Effort
KARNA WALTER   *85*

11   Undergraduate Research Revisited
Resources for Faculty and Opportunities for Students
LAURA DAMUTH   *93*

Notes   *103*

Appendices   *111*
     NAFA Foundation and Institutional Membership   *111*
     Competitive Scholarships, Opportunities,
     and Internships at a Glance   *119*

Index   *161*

Acknowledgments

The National Association of Fellowships Advisors (NAFA) conference in Washington, DC, in July of 2007 was perhaps NAFA's most ambitious undertaking. NAFA and Washington are a perfect pairing because many of the scholarship foundations have offices there, and the potential for partnerships with government agencies, embassies, and internship programs is extensive. Having the conference in the nation's capital also allowed interactions with a variety of government officials including individual meetings with U.S. senators and representatives. John Bader (Johns Hopkins University) arranged for panel discussions on foundation funding issues and the politics of government-funded scholarships. The conference opened with a lovely reception hosted by Sir David Manning, British ambassador to the United States (2003–2007), and his wife, Lady Catherine Manning, held in their home. Successful conferences require dedication on the part of a small group who assume large responsibilities. Special thanks in particular go to Paula Warrick (American University), who was vice president in 2007. The vice president is responsible for coordinating all aspects of the conference, including housing, special events, materials, panels, and speakers. Paula Warrick did a remarkable job, working collaboratively with a wide range of organizations and engaging actively a significant portion of the NAFA membership. Katherine Stahl, director of American University's Career Center, was very generous in providing additional staff support and other resources. Special thanks also go to Beth Powers (University of Illinois at Chicago), then president of NAFA, who worked extensively with scholarship and fellowship foundations and provided valuable experience from her work on previous NAFA events.

The Executive Board of Directors and Board members (see the appendices) were also major contributors to making the three-day conference a success. Additional conference planners include Shahrzad Arasteh (St. John's College), Josie Armenttrout (American University), Senem Bakar

(American University), Nancy Barker (American University), Brian Blair (American University), Monique Borque (Willamette University), Chris Bramwell (AMIDEAST), Nichole Burruss (University of Louisville), Betsy Bye (Truman Scholarship Foundation), Tineke Cunning (Pennsylvania State University), Laura Damuth (University of Nebraska, Lincoln), Elize Derstine (Truman Scholarship Foundation), Jim Duban (University of North Texas), Joan Echols (American University), Carolyn Emigh (Georgetown University), Janine Farhat (the College Board), Anjali Garg (Truman Scholarship Foundation), Anne Hamilton (American University), Kathleen Hearons (American University), Lisa Grimes (College of William and Mary), Jim Hohenbary (Kansas State University), Emily Horn (George Washington University), Ruth Keen (American University), Katherine Kirlin (American University), Christine Lam (American University), Jennifer Lin (Johns Hopkins University), Nancy Miller (University of Maryland, Baltimore County), Deirdre Moloney (George Mason University), Amanda Onysio (University of Illinois at Chicago), Linna Place (University of Missouri-Kansas City), Geri Rypkema (George Washington University), Rebecca Shakespeare (American University), Camille Stillwell (University of Maryland, College Park), Moira Tarpy (George Washington University), Alex Trayford (Wheaton College), Tonji Wade (Truman Scholarship Foundation), Karna Walter (University of Arizona), Susan Krauss-Whitbourne (University of Massachusetts Amherst), Carol Shiner-Wilson (Muhlenberg College), Debra Young (University of Mississippi) as well as Jane Morris (Villanova), John Richardson (University of Louisville), and Gordon Johnson (University of Cambridge and Provost of the Gates Cambridge Foundation).Tara Yglesias, Deputy Secretary of the Harry S. Truman Scholarship Foundation also provided countless hours of support.

Critical to the success of the conference was the cooperative support of foundation members. The list of those who contributed to the conference and continue to actively support NAFA and the students they serve is too long to include here. But a few provided support beyond what could be reasonably expected: Mary Denyer, Assistant Secretary, Marshall Aid Commemoration Commission; Frances Dow, Chair of the Marshall Aid Commemoration Commission; Mary Lou Hartman, Director, George Mitchell Scholarship Program; Walter Jackson, Program Manager, Fulbright U.S. Student Programs; Gordon Johnson, Provost, Gates Cambridge Trust; Jane Curlin, Senior Program Manager, Morris K. Udall Foundation;

Melissa Millage, Senior Program Manager, Morris K. Udall Foundation; Michael Lenardo, OXCAM Program Scientific Director, NIH Oxford Cambridge Scholars Program; Sharon Nishizaki, Senior Program Officer, NSEP David L. Boren Fellowships; Tom Parkinson, Beinecke Scholarship Program; Christopher Powers, Deputy Director, U.S. Student Programs, Institution of International Education; Patti Ross, Vice President of the Coca-Cola Scholars Foundation; Fred Slabach, Executive Secretary, Truman Scholarship Foundation; Renee Stephenson, The Rotary Foundation; Renee Stowell, Marketing Coordinator, British Counsel USA; Joshua Wyner, Chief Program Officer, Jack Kent Cooke Foundation; Tara Yglesias, Deputy Executive Secretary, Truman Scholarship Foundation; Lewis Larsen, Vice President and Director of programs, James Madison Memorial Fellowship Foundation.

Special thanks to Paul Clement, former Solicitor General of the United States, for delivering the keynote address in Washington, DC, and to Marianne Craven, Managing Director of Academic Programs, Bureau of Educational and Cultural Affairs, whose talk is included in these proceedings. Thanks go as well to all the conference presenters and to the staff of the University of Arkansas Honors College, especially Lance Owen (Associate Director of the Office of Post-Graduate Fellowships) and Nina Simmons (Honors College Office Assistant), for their proofreading help, and to Bryan Hembree (Director of the Office of Academic Scholarships) for the cover photo of the bronze statue of J. William Fulbright, created by sculptor Gretta Bader in honor of the 50th anniversary of the German-American Fulbright Educational Exchange Program. The support of University of Arkansas Chancellor G. David Gearhart and Honors College Dean Bob McMath also helped make this publication possible, as did the efforts of the University of Arkansas Press team: Larry Malley, Director; Brian King, Director of Editing, Design, and Production; and Julie Watkins, Assistant to the Director.

Introduction

Increasingly, universities across the country view the educational mission as extending beyond the classroom. Volunteer service programs, memberships in Campus Compact, and service-learning courses that have a community-based component are becoming commonplace. Study abroad has become an increasingly important educational tool. Universities advertise the percentage of their students who participate, understanding that studying abroad has the potential to provide a more intimate understanding of the world's political and economic complexities than can be gained in the campus classroom. Study abroad is no longer restricted to the few who can afford it as institutions raise funds to open the opportunity to more and more students. Undergraduate research is becoming the norm instead of the exception. Talented undergraduates across the country are getting involved in research earlier in their undergraduate careers. At state institutions, honors programs and colleges usually require some sort of capstone experience, if not a research-based thesis, and departments, especially in the sciences, often require a senior thesis of all their students. Universities are also working to break down the traditional boundaries between fields, as academic inquiry becomes more and more interdisciplinary. Students frequently find themselves majoring in one discipline, conducting research in another department, or working collaboratively across several departments. Given technological advances in the last several decades, available information on any given topic seems nearly unlimited, and mastering any subject in its entirety is becoming less and less possible. Learning how to frame questions, approach problems, think critically, and access appropriate information is becoming more important than ever, and often this kind of learning is enhanced by experiences beyond the traditional classroom.

Fellowship advisors help facilitate these experiences. Many advisors are faculty members who engage with students in the classroom, but faculty member or not, advising on fellowships is very much a teaching activity, and when done energetically and appropriately, it contributes to a university's mission of providing students with a broad, interdisciplinary education that prepares them to engage effectively in a developing world.

The National Association of Fellowships Advisors held its fourth biennial conference in Washington, DC, in 2007. *NAFA in Washington: Scholarships in a National Context* focused on student learning outside the classroom and how that engagement can help develop future leaders. Paul Clement, then solicitor general of the United States, discussed how his own experiences as a Marshall Scholarship candidate influenced his understanding of the importance of public service. NAFA also hosted an embassy and international foundations scholarship fair, as well as an internship fair. Many of the sessions led by faculty representatives dealt with advising as an educational enterprise: teaching students to write effective personal statements, advising students on reshaping a loss into an opportunity, developing models of faculty involvement in the process, integrating research and scholarship advising, establishing fellowship preparation courses on "enduring pedagogical and philosophical bases," expanding the core curriculum, and more.

The essays in this collection arise in large part from these discussions. The book's title, *Leading the Way: Student Engagement and Nationally Competitive Awards,* refers to the various groups involved in the scholarship process: foundations, universities, advisors, and (most importantly) the students they help educate. Providing opportunities for student engagement at the national and international levels increases understanding of global economic, social, and political issues. Universities and foundations both work to this end. Advisors provide information about and encourage participation in a variety of educational and service activities, while student leaders find and often create their own opportunities, embracing the chance to engage.

The first article in this volume is based on a keynote address by Marianne Craven, Managing Director of Academic Programs, Bureau of Cultural Affairs. In "State Department Initiatives for International Academic Exchange," she writes about the State Department's emphasis on partnering with key players in higher education, which resulted in the Summit of U.S. College and University Presidents on International Education. Former Harvard president Derek Bok, in *Our Underachieving Colleges*, outlines the current higher-education position on study abroad experiences. According to Bok, when study abroad lasts more than a semester, it usually produces important results, such as, "a lost parochialism, a greater realism about other societies, and an abiding sense of their complexity and the hazards of easy generalizations. There is evidence that education abroad can produce significant attitudinal changes as well: greater interest in world affairs, greater commitment to peace and international cooperation, and greater appreciation of the differing views and customs encountered in other nations."[1] He reports regretfully that while the number of students participating in study abroad continues to increase, only about 12% of undergraduates study overseas, with 70% of these staying for fewer than six months. Finally, "most of them choose countries reasonably similar to the United States. Britain is the leading choice, followed by France, Spain, Italy, and Germany."[2] Marianne Craven indicates that the Fulbright Program and other exchanges are sensitive to these higher-education concerns. Ten years ago these countries were top spots for Fulbright Scholars as well, but more recently there has been a shift to countries like Brazil, Indonesia, Pakistan, Russia, and China. New exchanges have also been created to expand opportunities. According to the Institute of International Education's 2008 Open Doors Report, the number of U.S. students studying in China, Argentina, South Africa, Ecuador, and India is up by 20% in each of these countries over the previous year.

The three chapters that follow Craven's are also written from a scholarship foundation perspective. Like advisors, foundations are part of the educational process (and not simply through the opportunities their funding provides). Applications themselves are teaching tools, as is vividly apparent in the Truman application. The Truman Foundation is well-known for leading the way in its appreciation for the process itself. The foundation hopes that its application will provide an opportunity for students to think through their service and leadership experiences, assess their goals, and develop a plan for implementing them. Even students who do not receive the scholarship have engaged in a valuable learning experience. Clearly, developing a better understanding of what leadership means is one of the Truman Foundation's major objectives. Tara Yglesias, Deputy Executive Secretary of the foundation, provides in "*Non Ducor, Duco*" invaluable advice for students (and their advisors) on how to understand and articulate leadership involvement. Students reading the chapter will quickly learn that at least for the Truman Foundation, leadership is not about leading by example or leading as part of a group or simply piling up a list of leadership titles.

Patti Ross (Vice President of the Coca-Cola Scholars Foundation) and her coauthors Mike Mallory (President, Ron Brown Scholar Program), Vanessa Evans (Associate Director, Ron Brown Scholar Program), and Colleen Quint (Executive Director of the Senator George J. Mitchell Scholarship Research Institute) discuss finding students with leadership potential as early as high school. These dedicated young people often excel academically while engaging actively in public service in college, making them potential applicants for competitive awards for graduate school a few short years later.

Michael Lenardo (National Institutes of Health OXCAM Program, Scientific Director) provides the final foundation chapter. His focus is "a new approach to biomedical PhD training." Lenardo was part of a team that helped launch an NIH-Oxford program in 2001 and then expanded it the next year to include Cambridge. The new approach focuses on melding the best practices from UK and U.S. graduate programs, moving students more quickly into hands-on, internationally collaborative, inter-disciplinary research of their own design.

Our volume continues with a chapter that all applicants for any award should read: "Understanding the Odds: A Reader's Perspective." Doug Cutchins provides an insider's look at what is finally a subjective process. A different group of readers, a different set of interviewers, might easily select a different set of recipients. Talented students abound; scholarship opportunities are by comparison few. Who of the many will be selected depends to some extent on the selectors. Students who are not selected and understand this will have less trouble coping with momentary defeat. Those who win will have a deeper sense of their good fortune.

The remaining chapters in the collection are written by fellowships advisors. Paula Warrick's "Creating Opportunities for Experiential Education in a Resource-Strained Environment" provides a select list of the kinds of out-of-classroom experiences that contribute to a student's overall educa-tion and suggests that a little research often unearths a variety of unex-pected opportunities.

Three of the chapters, Carol Shiner Wilson's "A Newcomer's Guide to Scholarship Advising," Lance Owen's "Preparing for *the* Interview: Advice from a Gates Cambridge Scholar and Fellowships Advisor," and Karna

Walter's "Involving Faculty in the Scholarship Process," address practical aspects of advising. All emphasize the opportunities advisors have to work cooperatively with other offices, to include faculty from a wide range of disciplines, and to expand students' educational experiences. In "Undergraduate Research Revisited," Laura Damuth, who both advises students on fellowships and directs the University of Nebraska's undergraduate research office, encourages advisors to connect students with undergraduate research opportunities, providing guidelines on how to begin. Lisa Knepshield addresses the important issue of diversity in scholarship applications. Foundations strive to be as inclusive as possible, but despite the best efforts of universities, advisors, and foundations, underrepresented group participation is still low. "Encouraged to Apply: Diversity and the Scholarship Process" looks at possible reasons for this at four institutions (large public, small private, urban, liberal arts) to determine common factors. That a problem exists is clear in all cases; possible solutions are less apparent.

I teach classes in our Honors College as well as English department courses on the literature of the American South, but some of my most meaningful teaching experiences have been across the table with students applying for graduate programs, research grants, or nationally competitive awards. Students applying for these awards tend to be curious, engaged, well trained, well informed, and committed to a particular vision or goal. Advising cannot and should not supplant the work of faculty, but should complement it. Universities, foundations, faculty, and advisors encourage students to stretch academically, engage civically, and think globally. Students who do this are not led, only assisted in finding their own way.

Suzanne McCray
University of Arkansas

1

State Department Initiatives for International Academic Exchange[1]

MARIANNE CRAVEN

Marianne Craven has served as Managing Director of Academic Programs, Bureau of Educational and Cultural Affairs (ECA), U.S. Department of State since 1999. She is a former Foreign Service officer who served overseas in Mali, Poland, and Italy. She previously was staff director for the ECA bureau, and currently holds the senior career civil service position in the Office of Academic Programs, which sponsors Fulbright Scholarships, Humphrey Fellowships, Gilman Scholarships, English-teaching programs, language study exchanges, community college scholarships, and overseas educational advising. These programs are active between the United States and more than 150 countries, funded at a level of over $300 million in fiscal year 2009. Ms. Craven also represents the State Department on higher education issues with UNESCO. She is a graduate of Smith College.

The U.S. higher-education community and advisors on nationally competitive awards are essential partners with the State Department, both in the Fulbright program and the related academic exchanges that we

1

sponsor. Over the past several years, we have worked to continue to strengthen our longstanding cooperation with U.S. higher education, a partnership that began when the Fulbright program was established over sixty years ago.[2]

As one example of that vibrant partnership, in a few weeks, the third joint delegation of U.S. college and university presidents and U.S. government officials will travel overseas to promote U.S. higher education to international audiences and also to encourage more study abroad by Americans. These delegations have met with government leaders, university rectors, business groups, and students to send the message that the United States welcomes international students in hopes of seeing more American students go abroad.

NAFA's primary focus is on fellowships for Americans, but I am also going to mention some of our exchanges for foreign students and educators. It will help give a more complete picture and context of our priorities for exchanges, and might suggest ways that academic institutions could take further advantage of the presence of foreign students on campus, sparking interest among Americans in applying for the Fulbright and other overseas study scholarships.

Educational exchanges are a very high priority for the Department of State. Former Secretary of State Condoleezza Rice was personally very committed to exchanges as a key element of the department's mission. She cosponsored our first-ever Summit of U.S. College and University Presidents on International Education, held at the State Department in January 2006.

The joint higher-education–government delegations—to East Asia in November 2006, South Asia in March 2007, and to Latin America—were one outcome of that summit, a landmark event for us that continues to define many of our priorities for educational exchanges as we look to the future.

Former Under Secretary of State Karen Hughes regularly described exchanges as the most important element of the State Department's public diplomacy efforts. My office, Academic Programs, houses the Fulbright program, Humphrey Fellowships, Gilman Scholarships, most of the State Department's National Security Language Initiative Scholarships for Critical Language Study, undergraduate programs for foreign student leaders, teacher exchanges, educational advising of foreign students abroad, and English-teaching programs.

Our programs also benefit from the strong support and commitment of the U.S. Congress, which has been very consistent in fostering and funding educational exchanges over the years. And of course, we have a wonderful worldwide network of stakeholders, advocates, and partners among foreign governments, alumni of Fulbright and other exchanges in the United States and over 150 countries, as well as the academic community, the private sector, and the nongovernmental organizations that assist in the administration of these exchanges.

The legislative mission for Fulbright and other exchanges is to promote mutual understanding between Americans and people of other countries. This remains the foundation of all our exchanges. At the same time, we seek to ensure that these exchanges are responsive and relevant to world issues and fulfill important long-term U.S. foreign policy goals. Over the past five years, we have made some major shifts in our exchanges, in response to the events of September 11, 2001. We created new exchanges and put many more resources into countries with significant Muslim populations, first in the Near East and South Asia, and then in East Asia and Africa. Our effort to assess and adjust priorities and support exchanges with countries where it is especially important to promote greater mutual understanding with the United States is a continuous and evolving process.

To illustrate some of the changes we have made, I have included a list of countries where we had the largest Fulbright programs in terms of participant numbers ten years ago, and then the list of the largest Fulbright programs today. Ten years ago the top ten Fulbright countries were Germany, the United Kingdom, Italy, Spain, France, Japan, Mexico, Argentina, India, and Austria. Today they are Germany, Russia, Pakistan, Indonesia, Turkey, China, Brazil, Mexico, Spain, and Korea.[3] These numbers only reflect our support for Fulbright exchanges and do not include new undergraduate student leader programs, critical language study institutes, or Gilman Scholarships.

Last month we hosted our largest-ever group of American Fulbrighters going to the Near East and South Asia—about 200 students and scholars—at a pre-departure orientation in Washington, representing a doubling in the size of that program over the past five years. We are gratified by the interest shown by American students and faculty applicants in going to these and other high-priority countries. I should note that, not surprisingly, there is still strong interest among our applicants in Western Europe and the developed, English-speaking world, where we have a strong Fulbright tradition, and our goal is to maintain effective and stable exchanges with all world regions.

We have created new programs to reach diverse students in Western Europe, from immigrant and other minority or disadvantaged populations, and indigenous minority students in Latin America, through undergraduate student leader institutes held on U.S. college campuses, teacher exchanges, and placement of American Fulbright English-teaching assistants in diverse and multicultural schools overseas.

The National Security Language Initiative has been a major priority for us since former President George W. Bush announced it at the U.S. University Presidents Summit in 2006. This year, 150 American Fulbright students will receive scholarship enhancements to take part in intensive study of Arabic, Russian, Chinese, South Asian languages, and other critical languages before beginning their primary Fulbright projects. About 200 Gilman undergraduate students are also studying in critical language countries. In 2006 we created a new summer Critical Language Scholarship Program, and 364 American students have received scholarships for overseas language study this summer. We received 6,000 applications for those 364 scholarships, so the interest among American students has been very high.

The State Department also brings Fulbright foreign-language teaching assistants to the United States to help teach critical and other important world languages on American campuses, including several young teaching assistants from Iran, and we support youth exchange and teacher exchange language study programs at the high school level.

Another major new area of emphasis over the past five years, encompassing all our exchanges, is the effort to reach younger and more diverse audiences, including disadvantaged populations, through programs that seek and promote academic excellence and leadership development.

We have created more exchanges at the undergraduate level especially for non-elite populations; supported outreach efforts to increase diversity of participation in exchanges like Fulbright; and created a new English-teaching initiative for disadvantaged high school students overseas, helping them acquire important skills while building a diverse pool of future candidates for our undergraduate and graduate exchanges. We have also developed new exchanges for educators who work with young people.

This effort to reach more young people through exchanges has extended to the Fulbright program as well. About five years ago we awarded approximately 900 scholarships to U.S. Fulbright students. In 2007 we awarded 1,400 scholarships to American Fulbright students. This expansion reflects an increase in our budget, but also a belief that we need to offer this life-changing exchange experience to more young people as they are making decisions about the direction of their careers.

Promoting diversity among American participants in our exchanges is also a very high priority. We are proud of the achievements of the Gilman Scholarship Program for American undergraduates with financial need, which includes high levels of participation by minority students.

We believe that the Gilman Scholarship is the most successful government or private program to include minorities in study abroad—the ratio of African American participants in Gilman is nearly four times the national rate of African Americans studying abroad (15 percent in Gilman vs. 4 percent overall), for Asian American Gilman recipients it is three times the national rate (18 percent vs. 6 percent), and the ratio of Hispanic Gilman recipients is more than double the national rate of Hispanic American students studying abroad (13 percent vs. 6 percent).

The proportion of Gilman recipients going to "nontraditional" countries also well exceeds that of the general U.S. study abroad population. The proportion of Gilman recipients who study abroad in Africa is more than double the national rate. For Asia it is nearly four times the national rate, and the proportion studying in the Middle East is five times the national rate. We are also making concerted outreach efforts in the Fulbright program to reach diverse student populations and have seen increases in both Fulbright application numbers and finalist numbers among minority students.

Through the Fulbright program, we also just launched a pilot effort with Music Television's college network MTVU—the Fulbright MTVU award—in which four American students (Aaron Schneyer, Georgetown University; Larnies Bowen, New York University's Gallatin School of Individualized Study; Phally Chroy, Temple University; and James Collins, Harvard University) in music fields have received Fulbright awards for overseas study. They reported on their experiences through broadcasts, blogs, and other media on the MTVU network on U.S. college and university campuses. We developed this program as a "public-private partnership" in recognition of the importance of music as a vehicle for international communication among young people and also to help raise awareness about overseas study opportunities among a diverse population of students on U.S. campuses.[4]

I mentioned our study institutes in the United States for undergraduate student leaders. Most of these programs are for foreign students, but one pilot initiative, the "fusion arts exchange," is bringing together foreign students with American peers at U.S. universities this summer to study together and collaborate on projects in four areas: digital media arts, screenwriting and film, sports management, and musical composition and performance.

In the music project, for example, students are coming from Brazil, South Africa, Mali, India, and Ireland to study with young American musicians at Northeastern University in Boston, which was selected through a grant competition to administer the music project.

We are delighted by the strong level of interest in exchanges and study abroad among Americans. The Open Doors study, which the State Department funds, has shown steady increases in the annual numbers of Americans studying abroad in recent years—over 200,000 in the last report.

International Education Week, which the State Department cosponsors with the U.S. Department of Education in November each year, is an opportunity to highlight the importance of international education and exchanges on campuses across the country and to showcase fellowship opportunities for international study, including the Fulbright and Gilman programs and critical language scholarships. We hope many institutions will participate in International Education Week and report on campus events through our Web site at exchanges.state.gov.

Finally, another overarching priority for our exchanges is to include and encourage community service and volunteer activities among our exchange participants, in both directions. We find that the dedication, energy, and interest in other cultures that inspires students and faculty to participate in international exchanges readily extends to their taking part in and leading community service and outreach activities, from assisting with disaster relief efforts to making school visits and participating in tutoring and service projects. We also encourage them to be active and engaged alumni.

American Fulbrighters and Gilman students are wonderful ambassadors of our country. We ask all Fulbright and Gilman students to be aware of their role in representing the ideals and values of the United States abroad while pursuing their overseas fellowship projects. Of course, I hope advisers will encourage their many outstanding and diverse students to apply to the Fulbright or Gilman programs and to make these their top choices for a fellowship. But we also appreciate the value of the many other fellowships offered to students at U.S. institutions.

When we participate with other countries in international higher-education discussions—at UNESCO, or in the context of the G-8 economic summit, or in other international fora—we are reminded again and again of the incredible quality, richness, diversity, and breadth of U.S. higher education, not the least of which are the myriad fellowship and scholarship opportunities that are available to students at our institutions.

And we always talk in these international meetings about the strengths of our higher-education system, which is based on the contributions and cooperation of many individuals and institutions in both the public and private sectors. So we are delighted that so many fellowships exist to serve different and complementary needs and goals, and that they reach many more students than our exchanges alone can do. We need to offer as many rewarding opportunities to young people as possible. At the same time, I hope advisors across the country remember the unique and life-changing experiences offered by Fulbright programs—perhaps most importantly, the chance to contribute to increasing mutual understanding between Americans and people from other countries.

2

Non Ducor, Duco
Leadership and the Truman Scholarship Application[1]

TARA YGLESIAS

Tara Yglesias has served as the Deputy Executive Secretary of the Truman Foundation for the past five years and has been involved in the selection of Truman Scholars since 2001. During this time, she had the opportunity to study the trends and characteristics of each incoming class of scholars. She used this knowledge to assist in the development of new foundation programs and initiatives as well as the design of a new foundation Web site and online application system. An attorney by training, she began her career by spending six years in the Office of the Public Defender in Fulton County, Georgia. She specialized in trial work and serious felonies but also assisted with the training of new attorneys. A former Truman Scholar from Pennsylvania, she also served as a Senior Scholar at Truman Scholars Leadership Week and the foundation's Public Service Law Conference prior to joining the foundation's staff.

Leadership is one of the core components of any successful scholarship application. Whether the student is interested in the arts, government service, medicine, or academic research, the student must be able to demonstrate that he or she will be an agent for change in the chosen discipline. This quality is what essentially convinces the committee that the student is a good investment—and that providing support to the student now will likely yield returns in the future.[2]

The Truman Scholarship lists leadership, along with a commitment to public service and intellectual achievement, as one of our three main criteria for selection. It is often easy for a student to identify and explain public service involvement. Providing information on intellectual achievement is also fairly straightforward. But explaining leadership is somewhat more elusive.

The Problem

Each year, the Truman Foundation offers faculty representatives feedback on the applications of those students not selected for interview. We provide this feedback in an effort to improve the applications that we receive. If each faculty representative is better equipped to understand our selection criteria, then these representatives will be better able to identify and assist appropriate applicants. We believe that the feedback process can also help to level the playing field for those faculty representatives who are either new to the process or unable to dedicate as much of their time to advising as they would prefer.

But feedback has another, more mundane, purpose. Feedback is the easiest way for the foundation to determine whether our message is clear. If we see a persistent problem, we may have identified an area where we need to refine our materials or better define terms for our applicants and faculty representatives.

In a typical year, we receive feedback requests on approximately 150 files.[3] The foundation reviews the files and then provides either written or verbal feedback to the faculty representative. There is often a dialogue between the foundation and the faculty representative as points are clarified and questions asked.

The foundation also makes a point of reviewing reader comments on approximately 150 files a year. The foundation conducts this review to ensure that our readers are rating applications appropriately. We also review the comments to ensure that we provide adequate training to the readers.

Those applicants for whom faculty representatives request an appeal are also reviewed. Faculty representatives can request an appeal on any student who is not selected for an interview. These applications are closely read, along with all reader comments. The foundation receives approximately 120 requests for appeal each year.

There is some overlap between these groups of files, but the foundation reviews approximately one-half of our unsuccessful files each year.[4] The overwhelming number of these files—approximately 85 percent—failed to advance to finalist status in part because of a lack of demonstrated leadership.

For the foundation, it is nearly impossible to determine whether this failure to advance resulted from an actual lack of leadership—or an inability to articulate leadership on the application. A look at how we at the Truman Foundation evaluate leadership may provide guidance for advisors as they assist applicants. An examination of prototypical responses to our leadership question may provide insight into the problems students face in articulating their exceptional contributions.

A Few Ground Rules

The guidelines outlined in this chapter apply only to the Truman Scholarship application process. There may be some nuggets of general applicability, but most of the comments presented here are tailored to our process. We are not responsible for the application of this material in untested scholarship settings.

Additionally, I do not mean to overemphasize the role of leadership in the Truman application process. Leadership is a major component of the Truman Scholarship, but it is not the only component of a successful application. Students with unusual or modest records of leadership can sometimes be successful in the Truman application process. Similarly, students with very impressive records of leadership—but more modest records of public service—are sometimes unsuccessful in the Truman application process.

Leadership on the Truman Application

The Truman application requests a short essay on an example of leadership (Question 7),[5] a letter of recommendation corroborating the student's leadership example, and a list of leadership roles within campus and public service activities (Questions 2 through 4). The Institutional Nomination Letter should also address the leadership abilities of the student, but in more general terms than the letter dedicated to this issue. The student can receive up to three points for his or her leadership record.

The readers review the application in the order presented in the online application process: Institutional Nomination Letter, student application, policy proposal, transcript, and letters of recommendation. The most critical part of the application—as it relates to the evaluation of a student's leadership—is the response to Question 7 contained in the application itself.

The first discussion of the student's leadership occurs in the nomination letter. Readers expect this letter to be fairly general—it is meant to serve as an introduction to the application—but they do expect to get a sense of the student's overall leadership abilities and potential. Successful nomination letters paint a picture of the rest of the application. For those applicants who have either nontraditional or modest leadership records, their faculty representatives should alert readers to this issue in the letter. This letter will provide an opportunity for the faculty representative to strengthen the case the student will make in his or her application.

The letter of recommendation on leadership should confirm the activity that the student chooses to write about in Question 7. The author need not be witness to the entire event; he or she only needs to be comfortable confirming the essential details. The most helpful letters explain the student's leadership style, putting his or her achievements in context. This letter can often provide details and relationships that the student will not have the opportunity to discuss in the response to Question 7.

The application asks for leadership roles in response to Questions 2 through 4.[6] Successful responses to these questions show an applicant who is adopting progressively increasing responsibility and involvement in activities that are important to the applicant. However, students often make the mistake of assuming that readers are familiar with every campus activity and every community organization. Successful applicants tend to offer information about their activities so readers can better understand both the activity and the student's role in the activity.

Most students have difficulty with the essay—and the essay is the most vital part of the leadership assessment. The essay is where the student articulates his or her leadership style. It is through this lens that the readers try to determine whether these leadership skills are likely to make the student a future agent for change.

Less-Than-Helpful Leadership Responses

Although we see a number of ineffective leadership responses, these responses tend to fall into one of five categories.

1. *"I did a great job!"* This essay usually involves the student performing a task that is part of an internship or other activity. The task is generally solitary—organizing an event or revamping a process— and much of the essay is spent with the student explaining the various challenges he or she encountered. The difficulty with this response is that the student never really displays leadership; he or she only displays competence.

2. *"It rubbed off on me!"* This essay generally describes a compelling example of another student's leadership. The student often follows an actual leader, generally in an elected office, and spends much of the essay explaining how he or she continued in the footsteps of this other, likely superior, student. This essay fails to articulate the leadership style of the applicant, serving only as confirmation that the student knows good leadership when he or she sees it.

3. *"I never met an office I didn't like!"* These applicants often have many leadership titles peppered throughout their application, but are not actual leaders. The telltale sign is that the student will be unable to cite a *single* compelling example of leadership in his or her essay. The student will try to work in multiple roles and examples to pad what is essentially the essay of an office placeholder. The problem with these applicants is that they often confuse titles with leadership. Simply occupying an office does not make the student a leader.

4. *"I lead . . . by example!"* This essay is usually seen in an application where there is a lot of public service but very little leadership. The student will often resort to explaining how he or she had an impact on an issue by doing something—generally solitary, but sincere nonetheless—not leading anyone. These essays not only fail to explain how the student can be a leader, but they also tend to be a red flag that leadership abilities of the applicant are rather thin.

5. *"There's no 'I' in team!"* This essay generally follows the exploits of a committee-led organization, a team of co-presidents, or a group of students. Although there may be individual leadership, the essay generally masks this by focusing on the activities of the group rather than the activities of the applicant. This essay often reflects the applicant's sincere belief that he or she did not accomplish anything alone. But readers tend to find these essays unhelpful. They know that the student appreciates the input of others, but would much rather be presented with a clear picture of the student's leadership abilities.

Helpful Leadership Responses

We see a variety of leadership roles assumed by successful Truman applicants. Some students may occupy traditional leadership roles on campus. Others may lead a grassroots movement. Still others are leaders in research or in the laboratory. Although the topics of these essays might be divergent, all of them tend to have the following elements:

1. *Identifies a significant problem.* Leadership examples are most compelling when the student writes about an issue that the student feels is important. The passion the student shows toward the issue not only comes out in the written application, but also in the interview. An essay on a matter to which the student is willing to dedicate his or her professional career is always more compelling than a piece on the importance of a balanced student government budget.

2. *Defined and unique role.* Simply put, the essay should be one that could only be written by the student. If the school has, for xample,

twenty student senators—and each one of them could produce a similar essay—the student should probably explore other options. Successful essays not only make the role of the student quite clear but also show how the student was the only person who could have fulfilled this leadership role.

3. *Participation of others.* In order for readers to assess the leadership of a student, the student needs to interact with others and explain how this interaction is a by-product of his or her leadership. Successful essays acknowledge the contributions of others but also show how the leader was able to utilize those contributions.

4. *Concrete outcome.* Successful essays tend to point to some concrete outcome as the result of the student's involvement. The scope of this outcome is somewhat immaterial, but the outcome should be defined and quantifiable. Students should avoid generalities such as "increased awareness" or "involved new students in the issue" unless these items can be quantified.

5. *Recent.* The readers are most interested in seeing an applicant who is getting more responsible and more involved with each passing year. The idea is that the student will be a tremendous future leader, not that he or she peaked in high school.

Articulating Leadership

Even with these guidelines, some students will still have a difficult time drafting a successful leadership essay. A few of these students might not have the necessary leadership abilities to produce a successful application. But the majority of students do have the necessary leadership abilities to produce a successful application. It may just take a bit of work to have the student seize upon the right leadership example. Some things to consider:

Thinking too narrowly. Students often equate leadership with an established title. Although students who occupy these offices can be leaders, they can also be mere holders of a title who demonstrate no leadership skills. Some of the most compelling leadership essays are written when a student sees a problem and steps in with a solution. Although the student did not have a title on which to base his or her authority, the student is recognized as an authority. Encourage students to think broadly about leadership and consider writing the essay about something other than occupying an office. The essay is really the only place on the application to articulate a nontraditional example of leadership; the students should take advantage of this opportunity.

Confusing change agent with facilitator. Although nontraditional examples of leadership are fine, students should take care not to conflate leadership with organization. Frequently, students will assume that providing a service, such as organizing an event or facilitating a heated discussion, is always an example of leadership. Although these activities can have elements of leadership, the student should be able to point to a way in which he or she *transformed* the process rather than just helped it along.

Toot! Toot! Many of the best Truman candidates are those students who are averse to blowing their own horn. These students spend a great deal of time thinking about others, and very little appreciating their own achievements. Although this quality is admirable, it tends to lead to essays that spend more time discussing the contributions of others or downplaying the role of the student. Some ground can be gained in the supporting letters, but it is much more interesting to the readers if the student can process his or her own leadership experience. These students will often need to be pushed to discuss their achievements. Question 7 is the *I/me* question of the application; readers are not interested in seeing the pronoun *we* in this essay. Question 8, on the other hand, is the place where the readers expect to see very little *I/me* and a lot of *we/they*.[7]

Millennials. The problem of modesty is somewhat complicated by a few of the more interesting elements of this particular generation. Many of these students think that leadership is a four-letter word. They take a dim view of students who are overly involved or who enjoy being singled out. Although all young people display a natural distrust of authority, this generation tends to reject both the authority figures as well as the systems. As a result, students often do not take advantage of leadership opportunities that are part of a recognized system. These students also tend to be very collaborative. They seek support from others and like to rule by consensus.

Collaborative leadership that displays a distrust of authority can be translated into a successful Truman application, but the student must recognize that his or her essay must appeal to a broad range of readers, including a few who come from generations that actually liked (or currently occupy) authority.

Articulating leadership in the Truman application is no easy task. Identifying an example of leadership will be difficult for many Truman applicants. These students tend to think of others before thinking of themselves. Expressing this leadership example is even more complicated. We ask students to be unique, relevant, and concrete, in 2,000 characters or less. Perhaps the easiest thing is to define leadership itself. For that we turn to a word from our sponsor:

"A great leader is a man who has the ability to get other people to do what they don't want to do . . . and like it."

Harry S. Truman

3

How Soon Is Too Soon?
Identifying Qualified Applicants

PATTI ROSS

Patti Ross is the Vice President of the Coca-Cola Scholars Foundation, which provides over $3.4 million in scholarships to over 600 students annually. Ms. Ross received her undergraduate degree from the University of Wisconsin-Madison and a Masters in Education in psychometry from Georgia State University. Having served in both the public and private school sectors and now with a focus on scholarships, she has worked with a range of professional organizations, bridging sectors including college counseling, advocacy, and the growth of private scholarship providers. Ms. Ross presently serves on several advisory boards, including FastWeb and the U.S. Public Service Academy as well as the Foundation Board for Georgia Perimeter College.

WITH VANESSA EVANS

Vanessa Evans is the Associate Director of the Ron Brown Scholar Program. Before joining the Ron Brown Scholar Program, Ms. Evans served as Senior Assistant Dean of Admissions at the College of William & Mary in Williamsburg, Virginia. Prior to that she served as Assistant Director of Admissions at James Madison University (JMU). In both capacities she focused on multicultural recruitment and recruitment programming. She currently serves on the Board of the National Scholarship Providers Association and the James Madison University Board of Visitors. She earned both a Bachelor of Business Administration and a Master's of Education in College Student Personnel Administration from James Madison University.

MIKE MALLORY

Michael Mallory currently serves as President of the Ron Brown Scholar Fund and Executive Director of the Ron Brown Scholar Program. Mr. Mallory launched the Ron Brown Scholar Program named in honor of Ronald H. Brown, former secretary of commerce, in 1996. Prior to that he worked in Undergraduate Admissions at the University of Virginia, where he earned a BS in Science Education and a MEd in Administration and Supervision. He was a classroom teacher in the Albemarle County public schools before being hired by UVA. His dedication to the Charlottesville community is evident through his work on numerous boards, including Computers 4-Kids, Urban Vision, and the Paramount Theatre Foundation. In addition, he has served as a member of the Board of Directors for the

National Scholarship Providers Association and as a Trustee of the College of Arts and Sciences Foundation of the University of Virginia.

COLLEEN QUINT

Colleen J. Quint is the Executive Director of the Senator George J. Mitchell Scholarship Research Institute. The Mitchell Institute is a nonprofit organization founded by Senator George Mitchell to provide scholarship assistance to Maine students and to research means of removing obstacles to higher education. The Mitchell Institute has provided over $6 million in scholarship support to over 1,500 Maine students to date. Mitchell Scholars receive numerous forms of personal support and professional development opportunities, and also participate in a longitudinal study of their experiences and outcomes. Ultimately the Mitchell Institute hopes to develop national models for effective scholarship programs and for improving access to college. Prior to her work with the Mitchell Institute, Ms. Quint spent ten years as an education attorney, working with high schools and colleges across the country on a wide variety of policy issues. Ms. Quint holds a BA from Bates College and a JD from University of Maine School of Law.

When Suzanne McCray, who served for three years on the Program Review Committee for the Coca-Cola Scholars Foundation's semifinalist reading committee, suggested that I contribute to a collection of essays on preparing students for nationally competitive awards, I immediately thought of several of my scholarship colleagues who would be excellent partners in sharing thoughts on this topic: Colleen Quint, executive director of the Mitchell Institute, and Mike Mallory and Vanessa Evans from the Ron Brown Scholar Program. Throughout the NAFA conference held in

Washington, DC, in 2007, when I heard descriptions of remarkable students, I thought participants could easily be speaking about one of our scholars. Students who receive our nationally vetted awards coming out of high school in turn often become high-achieving undergraduates who compete successfully again for competitive awards like the Rhodes, Marshall, Mitchell, Gates Cambridge, Fulbright, Truman, Goldwater, Udall, NSF, and more.

Included here is a description of the criteria we use to identify scholarship recipients, some of the services we provide in the ensuing years, and why ours are a likely corps of students for advisors at the undergraduate level to identify and work with on campuses across the country. In a sense we are representing the more than 150 organizations who are members of the National Scholarship Providers Association (NSPA, www.scholarshipproviders.org).[1]

On the two opportunities I have had to attend NAFA conferences, I was impressed by the dedication of its membership. Having been a high school counselor in my former life, I had what I always describe as the "great good fortune" to help shepherd high school students through the maze of college admissions to the joy of appropriate matches. NAFA is a uniquely rich group, because although individual members do not always have the opportunity to rejoice with the golden ring, the charge to encourage students to value process expands both the role and the importance of the profession.

Here is a note from a Coca-Cola Scholar who is presently working through that process:

> *Despite all of the structure of the process, it is largely self-driven. You get out what you put into it. I have invested a lot of time into this process, and even if I don't win a scholarship, I will still consider the process a HUGE success in my personal and professional development. I have been forced to think critically about my future . . . not just five years down the road, but ten, twenty, and even thirty years down!*
>
> —Rajiv Srinivasan, Coca-Cola Scholar, 2004

For the first two years of our program in 1989 and 1990, we actually asked our applicants to contemplate what their lives might be like in 2010. We asked them to project themselves forward and describe what they expected to be doing then. *"What do you think will be the major issues facing you, our country, and our world . . . and what part do you want to play in helping to resolve or affect these issues?"* we inquired. Having recently read more than 250 of these essays, I recognize that many of our scholars begin laying the groundwork for their futures during that pivotal time of late adolescence. Part of their success is that they formulate long-term goals along with the wisdom to rework those goals as needed. Without wishing away their undergraduate years, they are tuned into potential opportunities and at least welcome information that might be fruitful upon graduation.

The Ron Brown Scholar Program has published an amazing collection of essays written by their scholars as part of their scholarship application in *I Have Risen: Essays by African American Youth*.[2] Executive Director Mike Mallory notes: "The stories are gritty, poignant, honest, and inspirational." I was especially struck by the lack of self-pity, maturity of insight, enormous capacity to recognize the value of their backgrounds and the energy they project for moving forward. Antonia J. Henry is both a Ron Brown Scholar and a Coca-Cola Scholar. The opening paragraph of her essay—written when she was seventeen—is just one example of provocative, yet sound, writing:

> *The ignorance, misunderstanding, and prejudice of racism are steadily unraveling the fabric of America. As my generation matures, political correctness is seen as the panacea for this horrible disease. Yet, honest discourse must occur for members of different races to move towards acceptance of diversity.*

More than a description of racism, Antonia's insight suggests that *discourse* might improve conditions. Our scholars have already toyed with *problem solving* by the time we meet them; advisor encouragement can enhance that extraordinary skill, for one never knows a particular mentor or time that may be the catalyst for meaningful growth. Antonia, now a doctor, is participating in a surgical rotation at Brigham and Women's Hospital in Boston, Massachusetts.[3]

All of our programs look for students who are capable of helping to fulfill our missions; they are selected during their senior year of high school. Below is a general overview of the three scholarship programs.

Senator George J. Mitchell Scholarship Research Institute[4]

The core mission of the Senator George J. Mitchell Scholarship Research Institute is to increase the likelihood that young people from every community in Maine will aspire to pursue and achieve a college education. Selection is based on academic promise, financial need, and a history of community service. Mitchell Institute programming includes research and support services that create ongoing scholar involvement in leadership and professional development, as well as community service, professional and career development, and mentoring activities. Mitchell Scholars are largely first-generation college-goers from families with incomes at or below the state median. Despite these and other barriers, Mitchell Scholars graduate from college at the remarkable rate of 95 percent. And each year the Mitchell Scholars collectively provide over 17,000 hours of community service to their respective home states.

Colleen Quint offers this comment:

> *A number of our Mitchell Scholars have applied for and some have received prestigious graduate fellowships. Our experience with our scholars tells us that even the most ambitious and confident among these students can often be unaware of opportunities that exist, unsure of what resources might be available to them, and unconvinced that they are "good enough" for further recognition and support. If campus advisors to national fellowship programs were able to identify and reach out to Mitchell Scholars on their campuses, it could open a world of opportunity to them.*

Ron Brown Scholar Program

The mission of the Ron Brown Scholar Program is to identify and embrace exceptional African American students from low-income households who understand the value of service to others and have chosen to make this a lifetime commitment. The Ron Brown Scholar Program is not just a mechanism to finance needy, talented students, but also an ever-evolving institution whose goal it is to link permanently these dedicated and gifted youngsters to each other and the resources that will enable them to fulfill their dream of service and share their gifts with communities. Support is provided through professional and personal mentors, internships, job opportunities, national service initiatives, conferences, alumni participation, enrichment workshops, and ongoing communication and input to the program.

Vanessa Evans at the Ron Brown Scholar Program conveys the feelings of many scholarship providers who are attached to these students emotionally and financially, and who want the very best for them:

We think it is critical to begin the process with students early with regard to opportunities for fellowships like the Rhodes, Marshall, and Truman programs. The more information students are able to gather and the more clearly they understand the processes that lie before them, the more likely they will apply and shape their college experiences to put them in a more competitive position. Having advisors on campus to help guide their decisions is essential and beneficial not only to the student, but also to the colleges. Working with scholarship programs to identify our students on their campuses gives the scholarship program immediate access to a very talented pool of students, who typically will attend graduate school and/or seek out fellowship programs. More than 50 percent of our Ron Brown Scholars attend graduate school.

Coca-Cola Scholars Foundation

The Coca-Cola Scholars Foundation is an achievement-based scholarship program. Students are identified during their senior year of high school based on academics as well as school and community leadership. Like our fellow scholarship providers, the Coca-Cola Scholars Foundation continues to develop networking, internship, service, and job opportunities. As we move closer to our vision of being a powerful global network of world and community leaders, the scholars themselves are working with us, in person and through technology, to enhance these relationships on many levels. In 2007 the scholars established an Alumni Advisory Board. Their first major initiative was to raise funds through the scholar network to fund a National Coca-Cola Scholar.

Numbers often speak for themselves, and for the last several years— since we moved to an electronic application for the first phase of our application process—over 200,000 students access our Web site during the months of September and October when the application comes online. The next phase demonstrates self-selection—80,000 high school seniors actually complete the application. From this pool the foundation identifies 2,100 semifinalists through a quantitative scoring method. The semifinalists then complete an application, which requires official school documentation, two recommendations, and several short essays along with the expected lists of school activities, leadership opportunities, and community service projects.

The reading committee of thirty educators convenes in Atlanta to read the semifinalist applications and determines the 250 finalists who are interviewed in Atlanta to determine the level of their award: $20,000 for fifty of the scholars and $10,000 for two hundred. These Coca-Cola Scholars will benefit from $3 million in scholarship awards. It stands to reason that this diverse group of students, representing every state and socioeconomic category, has its superstars, having come through an ever-narrowing pipeline.

I cannot attest to the accuracy of the following comment from one of our Coca-Cola Scholars, but in light of the previous chronology of our process, I offer it as one opinion:

> *I have gotten to know a good chunk of my Rhodes class, and the impression that I have is that about eight members are just incredibly, incredibly amazing people and would probably get the Rhodes four out of every five times they applied for it. The rest of us have some unique interest or distinction, but you could really replace us with almost any of the district finalists. I think there is very little difference between most of the people who won at the district level and the people who didn't, and that those who win are just fortunate. There are steps you take to increase the probability that you'll win, but unless you're one of those eight people in the country, nothing is guaranteed.*
>
> —Dave Chokshi, Coca-Cola Scholar, 1999

None of our programs see the scholarship as the end of our relationship, but instead as the very beginning as we work to be one of their touchstones. Through our communications we provide our scholars with basic information about many of the nationally competitive scholarships available at the undergraduate and graduate level, but this is where we pass the baton to university and college fellowship advisors. We are, however, often asked to write letters of recommendation:

> *I actually learned about distinguished scholarships through UNC's Office for Distinguished Scholarships. My lead interviewer for the Morehead is the director (and a professor on campus) of this program. I met with him when I first arrived on campus freshman year and then occasionally over the past two+ years. We would discuss in brief thirty-minute sessions what I was doing on campus, what I wanted to major in, any thoughts I had about graduate school, etc. He focused my attention on applying for the Truman this year because it fit well with my interests and work on and off campus. He has guided me through most of the process thus far—editing essays, and requesting recommendations. If not for his support and guidance, I doubt I would be applying for this scholarship.*
>
> —Danielle M. Allen, Ron Brown Scholar, 2005

My process was rather simple (and standard for a Harvard undergrad). The process didn't start in full until the fall of my senior year. Unofficially though, I went on my own to the Office of Career Services to talk with a fellowships counselor. I also began talking to students who previously applied for post-graduate fellowships—any and all information was helpful. But by my senior year, I worked with a designated fellowships advisor to work through all the logistics of applying (particularly for the Rhodes and Marshall). We had to get Harvard endorsements to apply for both of those, so everyone was working with the University to get their materials together. In the end, I applied for four fellowships (Rhodes, Marshall, Fulbright, and Harvard-Cambridge—the one I won in the end). I was a Rhodes state finalist and a Marshall regional finalist.

—A. Damian Williams, Ron Brown Scholar, 1998

One thing is certain—there is no way to go through this intense application process, which requires so much self-analysis, without at times questioning the process itself. One of our Coca-Cola Scholars explains it this way:

There's also been a general underlying theme here about over-preparation. I'll admit that I find the whole process of grooming yourself to be a good Rhodes candidate a little bit distasteful, so you might want to take my advice with a grain of salt. Having said that, I think that one of the reasons I might have stood out among the district finalists was because I came across as less polished than some of the other finalists. . . . [M]y point is that a great deal of grooming and preparation is not a necessary condition for winning.

—Dave Chokshi, Coca-Cola Scholar, 1999

Dave provided us with a number of valuable insights about working with advisors or other interested parties:

First, do not let other people edit your statement so much that it is no longer personal. I only had a total of three people seriously look at my statement, and I only incorporated the comments of two of those three. A lot of that was because of time constraints, but a lot was also because I firmly believed that I knew how I wanted to portray myself. The function of reviewers should be to ensure that it is coherent.

Theresa Bridgeman (Coca-Cola Scholar, 1999) considers it chancy to structure courses and life at college to be more competitive for a specific award:

In general, I think it's a good idea for undergraduates to focus on their academic and extra-curricular interests without focusing too much on what "should" be done to get a "prestigious scholarship," at least during their fresh-man and sophomore years. While some prior preparation and an idea of the general requirements (such as GPA, etc.) is undoubtedly useful, it seems that students who try from very early stages to pack their resumes or pick their classes in order to get a scholarship are less successful applicants, and if they are selected they may be somewhat less happy with the experience (for exam-ple, Rhodes Scholars who go to Oxford to "be a Rhodes Scholar" rather than because there is a particular graduate degree program they particularly want to pursue). Getting feedback on the actual application and the application process is a useful—if unnecessary—component of winning one of these scholarships, but advising much younger students on how to gear their col-lege careers towards such scholarships may even be counterproductive. That said, closer to the time of application, it's always helpful to have someone read through essay drafts (and do a mock interview if at all possible). I have often helped younger students through that part of the process in much the same way as I received help.

One of the consistent threads between our programs and those at the graduate level is clearly community service. All of our applications require students to communicate how they might be making a difference in their communities, and from our follow-up with them, we know that they continue to stay involved on their college campuses. Many of the overseas programs foster improved understanding between people and countries, while our scholars, during high school, often bridge the gaps in their home communities between neighborhoods and schools. The distance some of our students travel both philosophically and in actual miles, from small rural towns to large urban cities and vice versa, is as far a journey and a cultural challenge as recipients experience overseas. One could make the assumption that many of our scholars come to col-lege with a level of self-awareness, understanding of social responsibility, and tools for collaboration that give them a head start. They know something about adjusting to new situations and the art of being flexi-ble, the intrinsic value of community service, and the tenets of team-work and leadership.

Next we asked several of our scholars to tell us about working with an advisor:

I do not remember my advisor being "officially appointed," but I worked with my German professor, who encouraged me to apply in the first place. Throughout the process, however, there really was not a lot of collaboration.

The professor encouraged me, pointed me down the path, and then it was up to me to write the essays and fill out the forms. In addition to my professor/advisor, the campus career planning center that helped with applying for fellowships. This group provided support on critiquing my essays before submission to Fulbright, and I found it very helpful. . . . The process was stressful at the time, but looking back on it, it really wasn't nearly as stressful as, say, applying to college in the first place.
—Mark Lutte, Mitchell Scholar, 1999; Fulbright Scholar, 2003

I won a research Fulbright to the UK in 2001. While at Bowdoin, I applied for a couple of internal scholarships and got to know the dean of students pretty well through that process. She was also in charge of the Fulbright applications for Bowdoin, and asked me during my senior year if I was interested in applying. She was helpful in managing the application process: assuring that I was on track for the filing deadline, coordinating recommendations, and providing school support through the application process. The one thing that really helped me win the Fulbright, I think, was that I had been in contact with the pre-eminent scholar in the UK on the topic I researched, and I got him to write a letter supporting my application as well as an admission offer from the University of York. The other fifteen or so UK Fulbrights that year seemed to have similar relationships with professors/institutions. That would be my key advice.
—Chris Stearns, Mitchell Scholar, 1997; Fulbright Scholar, 2001

Another question that we asked had to do with individual timelines surrounding the process. Some of these comments might cause advisors to grimace, but it seems reasonable that some of the most viable candidates might also be some of the busiest. Dave Chokshi agrees:

Finally, to those who are reading this in August of their senior year and are unsure about whether or not they should apply (I was in that position), I would strongly recommend going ahead with the application. As clichéd as it is, you will learn a lot about yourself in the process, and if you win, you will be part of a wonderful community for two years (and part of a pretty incredible network for the rest of your life). I hesitated because I didn't think I had a realistic shot at winning, and looking at it objectively, I probably didn't. You never know what will happen given the quirks of the process.

I did not find out about the Truman Scholarship until the beginning of my junior year at Stanford, and worked on the application just a few months in advance. . . . The mock interviews Stanford put together before the finalist interviews were particularly helpful.
—Theresa Bridgeman, Coca-Cola Scholar, 1999

Dave and Theresa are both Rhodes Scholars. What can we take away from these limited, though valuable, comments from scholarship administrators and scholars from the Mitchell Institute, the Ron Brown Scholar Program, and the Coca-Cola Scholars Program? Timelines and the level of involvement by faculty advisors vary as do the ways students approach their academic programs and seek assistance. And yet the sense of self that propels some of our strongest scholars forward is indicative of those who generally embrace feedback as long as it is not philosophically altering.

I remember vividly two of my most eager and thoughtful high school students who submitted their college application essays for me to read. It happened more than twenty-five years ago—but it seems like yesterday. I suggested they both rework their essays, providing clarity, adding examples, and so on, but after one or two revisions, they both approached me on the same day to say, "Mrs. Ross, this is it! I am finished." Students (and their advisors) know when the application is ready to ship.

This past year, after attending the NAFA conference in DC, I sent an e-mail to our 1,000 college-age scholars, letting them know of the availability of advisors on many campuses who assist students with prestigious scholarship applications. I referred them to the NAFA Web site to identify that person on their campus. I also provided to most of the advisors at the conference the names of Coca-Cola Scholars on their campuses. Why not? Some students will be ready to explore these opportunities early on while others already have these fellowships in their opportunity queue. The important students to reach are those who are unaware of these opportunities, as Colleen Quint pointed out earlier.

There are many benefits to identifying potential candidates early in order to provide important guidance to students who may not have it or know where to look for it otherwise, such as first-generation college-goers. Involvement with these students may not always result in successful applicants, but it will certainly help provide shape to their undergraduate study. Many colleges have an identification process in place; scholarship programs like ours, that identify talented students as early as high school, can also serve as another means of finding talented, engaged students. Successful applicants of nationally competitive awards at the undergraduate and graduate level and those in our programs often possess common characteristics: a willingness to take risks, a desire to be an agent for positive change, a strong work ethic, and a sense of service.

In closing I would like to share a portion of a report by one of our scholars written after his sophomore year of college. One might think that this is an isolated example, but Lee's experience speaks clearly to a significant percentage of the population whom we support through our programs:

Last summer I embarked on a trip that revolutionized the way I see the world and how I want to spend my time here. China is a country of vast extremes. There is extreme poverty and wealth, extreme happiness and unhappiness. The Chinese culture is immensely different from our own, and because of that I am drawn to it. While in China, I assumed the role as an educator for the first time in my life. I have had numerous experiences teaching children skills such as soccer and baseball. However, nothing could have prepared me for the conditions I found myself in once in China. For five weeks, I was responsible to fill five hours each day, five days a week, with material that would help set my students apart from other Chinese children that chose not to attend our summer camp. We had no curriculum, and no resources such as paper, paint, and books. We only had a blackboard and the collective ingenuity of twenty college-age students. Unlike any other experience in my life, my leadership abilities were tested and strengthened . . . [Back in the States] [f]or the past year, I have served as an intern for the program to create the curriculum that will be carried out by the teachers this year and in the years to come. I have created a 200-page teaching companion that will be implemented this year.

—Lee Sullivan, Coca-Cola Scholar, 2005

Lee's next project is a trip to Mount Everest Base Camp to raise the necessary funds to help address the troubled schooling conditions in a small village in Nepal:

I have never been so excited about a trip in my life, and it is still a year away. To go to this village and help them rebuild their school and see first-hand how our hard work will help these people is what motivates me.

Isn't this a young man you might like to meet? Nationally competitive awards for incoming freshmen and other undergraduate scholarships include many such students. If advisors are looking for talented students, they should not forget those who have already been vetted by very competitive programs. Providing guidance and support to these students will lead to even greater success for them and for their universities.

Scholar Contributors (and where they are now):

Danielle M. Allen (2005 Ron Brown Scholar, 2008 Truman Scholar) is completing her degree at the University of North Carolina at Chapel Hill, with a double major in Public Policy and Economics.

Theresa Bridgeman (1999 Coca-Cola Scholar, 2001 Rhodes Scholar) is a student at New York University School of Law, a first-year Root-Tilden-Kern Scholar, and an Institute for International Law and Justice Scholar.

Dave Chokshi (1999 Coca-Cola Scholar, 2001 Rhodes Scholar) is a student at the University of Pennsylvania School of Medicine.

Dr. Antonia J. Henry (1998 Ron Brown and Coca-Cola Scholar) is in residency at Brigham and Women's Hospital in Boston, Massachusetts.

Mark Lutte (1999 Mitchell Scholar, 2003 Fulbright Scholar) is currently a candidate for a Master's of Public Administration at The George Washington University in Washington, DC. He is also working as a contract specialist for the United States Mint.

Rajiv Srinivasan (2004 Coca-Cola Scholar) is a graduate of United States Military Academy and presently serves as the Academy Administrative Officer for Cadet Field Training at Fort Knox, Kentucky.

Lee Sullivan (2005 Coca-Cola Scholar) is attending the University of Colorado at Boulder.

A. Damian Williams (1998 Ron Brown Scholar) is completing clerkship with Supreme Court Justice John Paul Stevens.

4

The National Institutes of Health/Oxford/ Cambridge Scholars Program
A New Approach to Biomedical PhD Training

MICHAEL J. LENARDO

Michael Lenardo graduated with a BA from Johns Hopkins University and an MD from Washington University in St. Louis. He performed clinical work in internal medicine and research at the University of Iowa and received postdoctoral training at the Whitehead Institute for Biomedical Research at MIT with Nobel laureates David Baltimore and Philip Sharp. He established an independent research unit at the Laboratory of Immunology at the NIH in 1989 and became a senior investigator and section head in 1994. Dr. Lenardo serves on several editorial boards and has given numerous lectures around the world on his work on the molecular regulation of immune homeostasis. His work focuses on lymphocyte apoptosis, autoimmunity, and HIV pathogenesis. Along with Professor Sir John Bell and Professor Sir Andrew McMichael (both at Oxford University), he developed the NIH-Oxford Program in 2001. He then worked with Sir Keith Peters to establish the NIH-Cambridge Program in 2002.

In 1999 the National Institutes of Health (NIH) began an exciting experiment in biomedical research education.[1] Professors Harold Varmus and Michael Gottesman established the NIH Graduate Partnerships Program (GPP), which opened the intramural laboratories of the NIH to doctoral trainees. The GPP was designed to create a graduate student community by forging university partnerships for the training of doctoral bioscience students. The NIH has both an extramural division (approximately 90 percent of NIH resources are dispensed as grants to research institutes and universities) and an intramural division (approximately 10 percent of NIH resources support its in-house laboratories). The NIH intramural program, which includes the GPP, comprises over 1,500 research groups spanning the full spectrum of biomedical research. It is the largest medical science research enterprise in the world and is housed in Bethesda, Maryland, and several satellite campuses.

The organizational structure of the GPP is similar to that of a university, with the GPP director serving as the equivalent of a dean by overseeing various academic programs focused in thematic areas of research. The GPP sponsors graduate-student retreats, student research days, a graduate-student council, and other programs that foster an academic environment similar to that found at a university. These activities promote student interaction, help students solve problems during their training, and create an interactive graduate-student community on the NIH campus.

For the GPP vision to become reality, NIH leaders forged partnerships with outstanding university partners, work that involved both challenge and opportunity. The challenge involved building programs that would be regarded as "win-win" situations for university partners and NIH. Since its creation in the late 1930s, the Bethesda campus of NIH has been a haven for advanced trainees, including postdoctoral fellows, clinical fellows, and other professional scientists. Nevertheless, a 1999 survey conducted during the GPP planning process found that over 150 trainees had established ad hoc agreements with NIH faculty members to carry out all or part of their doctoral graduate work on campus. Thus a sizable population of doctoral trainees was already at NIH. In addition, in the mid-1990s intramural NIH created the postbaccalaureate ("postbac") program. This enabled students finishing bachelor's degrees to carry out full-time research at NIH for one or two years. The postbac program did not grant degrees, but it enabled students to burnish their scientific skills for future training in graduate or medical school. In effect the postbac program created a direct demand for a pathway that would allow students to earn a doctorate by continuing their NIH work. With these favorable antecedents for a formal graduate training program already in place by the end of the 1990s, the creation of the GPP seemed a logical next step.

The first new partnership launched by NIH was the NIH-Oxford Program in 2001. This partnership was launched by Professor John Bell and Professor Andrew McMichael at the University of Oxford and me. The following year the partnership was extended with the help of Professor Sir Keith Peters to include the University of Cambridge. Both partnerships came to be managed together as the NIH/Oxford/ Cambridge Scholars Program. Foremost in our minds was how to create an attractive program—attractive to the universities and their faculties, attractive to top-quality students, and attractive to the intramural scientists and leadership of NIH. We also had a strong motivation, given that NIH is the world's largest biomedical research enterprise, to create a unique opportunity for the most promising biomedical research students. We wanted to help these individuals develop the focus and skills that would enable them to make major biological and medical discoveries as successful twenty-first-century researchers.

We first examined biomedical graduate education in the United States. This revealed some surprising, and not altogether propitious, trends. First, we discovered that, among the thousands of biomedical doctoral programs already in existence, there was wide variation in oversight of content and attention to the needs of individual students. We found there was a conservative structure in most existing programs. Almost all programs required that students complete one to two years of didactic coursework and laboratory rotations, followed by four to eight years of thesis work. According to a National Research Council report, the average time to complete a degree for a U.S. biomedical research doctorate was 7.8 years and had steadily increased over the past twenty years. This, together with the American custom of three to five years of postdoctoral training, contributes importantly to delayed career development.

The NIH has determined that young investigators do not achieve their first independent faculty positions until their mid-thirties and are, on average, forty-two years old when they are awarded their first NIH

RO1 grants. Graduate students are largely the responsibility of individual faculty members. To these faculty members, the students often have dual roles in research efforts. On one hand students are "scientists in training" to be mentored in the practices of the discipline. On the other hand students represent the most inexpensive form of skilled labor available to universities and research institutes. These forces can contribute to the progressively increasing time that PhD students spend in training.

As we continued with our review of biomedical research training programs, we uncovered issues in the academic substance of the programs. These trends were difficult to quantify but on the whole led us to wonder if a new approach could be developed to prepare students to succeed as scientists in the twenty-first century. Given the increasing emphasis on collaboration and multidisciplinary approaches, we reasoned that it might be beneficial to incorporate these approaches into individual thesis projects. Also, given the increasingly global nature of biomedical investigation, we envisioned that a unique type of training could be developed that placed a strong emphasis on international work. Moreover, the model of master-apprentice that dominates graduate education appeared to confine students to a subordinate role throughout the course of their training at most institutions. There was a perception that leadership skills and management expertise could be acquired in postdoctoral training or on-the-job as a tenure-track faculty member, but that these proficiencies were not essential for doctoral students. Encouraging students to take charge of their projects seems to be a valuable approach that might succeed with capable students.

Finally, students received little exposure to how their work could intersect with the broader social fabric as a fundamental aspect of bioscience graduate training. Students seemed to go through grad school with little or no exposure to commercial, ethical, intellectual property, or political issues related to their research. There is an anachronistic tradition that commercial or practical applications of research are not within the scope of doctoral training. This is surprising given that many faculty members are involved in commercial enterprises. In addition the increasing prominence of the biotechnology industry has led to an increasing proportion of student trainees aiming toward careers in industry. While continuing to value fundamental, hypothesis-driven basic research, we imagine that it would be valuable to edify students about the forces that shape biological research and its applications outside of the university. Given these considerations, we set out to create a new approach to doctoral training.

Because there was no strong traditional model of graduate education at NIH, we were fortunate to be able to start from scratch. One priority was to make the program international. In that regard we were fortunate to find willing partners in Oxford and Cambridge universities in Great Britain. These two institutions reflect the different training approach for doctoral students usually employed in European countries. First, there is much less emphasis on didactic training and a greater emphasis on students getting into the lab faster, beginning thesis projects right away, and learning independently. Second, degrees in Britain typically take only three years.

However, this norm is largely dictated by a lack of funding for additional years of research rather than by pedagogical reasons. This feature influences other aspects of the graduate training experience in the United Kingdom. There are no rotations in most cases and no sense that the student must complete a cohesive project as a qualification for graduation. Although we would not necessarily concur with some of the underlying assumptions and practices in the United Kingdom, its andragogical philosophy provides a much more flexible format upon which to build a new type of program to suit exceptional American students. Third, students in the United Kingdom are given substantial independence in determining the focus and direction of their research. Fourth, there are distinctive and natural ties to international science in Europe and in other countries, particularly in the areas of infectious disease and tropical medicine. Finally, Oxford and Cambridge also provide strong collegiate systems that nurture microcosms for student interaction across academic disciplines. There are many advantages to Oxford and Cambridge Universities serving as international training grounds for students, including the fact that there is no language barrier (apart from colloquialisms) for American students.

With this background in mind, we set about to create an exciting, innovative program that would blend the best of American and British doctoral training. Because we want students to have the benefit of research environments in both the United States and the United Kingdom, we structure the program so that every student works on a collaborative project to be guided by a mentor in a lab at Oxford or Cambridge, as well as a mentor in an NIH intramural laboratory. We allow flexible choice of mentors with an emphasis on formulating a unified project to which each mentor contributes. Students spend half of their time in the UK laboratory group and the other half in the NIH lab. This approach has provided extraordinary experiences for students and an unparalleled opportunity to learn and observe different scientific approaches. We extend the flexibility even further by allowing for collaborative international projects involving additional mentors, laboratories, or countries, bringing further unique dimensions to the research. For example, students can work in Africa on AIDS vaccines, investigate SARS pathogenesis in laboratories in China, or study advanced microscopic techniques in Germany. The program administration provides the necessary logistical and travel support as well as academic advising to help the students navigate complex projects.

So how has this educational experiment fared after seven years? At present the NIH/Oxford/Cambridge Scholars Program has an enrollment of over eighty exceptional students and has graduated over twenty PhD students. The students entering the program have high GRE scores (above the ninetieth percentile) and an average GPA of approximately 3.8. Students initially find knitting an international collaboration to be intimidating, but as they progress in the program, with guidance they develop the requisite leadership and management skills.

We have established an elaborate advising system that is instrumental in keeping students on track through personal and scientific difficulties. A major unanticipated benefit of dual mentor projects is that they promote, by necessity, collaborative interactions between institutions and stimulate novel interdisciplinary relationships. In many instances we find that these collaborations extend beyond a student's thesis to other projects in the participating laboratories. It is a horizon-expanding experience for everyone involved. We have also found that students are taking advantage of international research opportunities in many parts of the world, especially throughout Great Britain.

We have found that our new training format is especially appealing to students seeking combined MD/PhD training. In support of our belief that investigators with combined MD/PhD training are better equipped to operate at the intersection between clinical medicine and laboratory research, Dr. Richard Siegel and I created the first NIH intramural MD/PhD program, which has allowed NIH-Oxford and Cambridge Scholars to matriculate simultaneously at one of the forty-two medical schools with an NIH-funded Medical Scientist Training Program

(MD/PhD program). Now three years old, this program offers students much of the same flexibility that the PhD students have in terms of crafting a curriculum for their doctoral thesis projects. It is anticipated that most will follow the recommended path of completing two didactic years of medical school prior to initiating their PhD research. The medical degree would be conferred by the participating medical school, and the PhD would be conferred by either Oxford or Cambridge. This new initiative further expands the partnership concept between NIH, domestic medical schools, and British universities. In summary the NIH/Oxford/Cambridge Scholars Program has proven to be an attractive and innovative training format that we believe provides students a unique, twenty-first-century training opportunity.

We anticipate that this experiment will continue to evolve. This year we will inaugurate the entry of students from the United Kingdom and the European Union in a special alliance between the National Institutes of Health and the Wellcome Trust. Perhaps the most important conclusion we have made so far is that, for the program to continue to be successful, it must remain flexible and prepare students to adjust to new and future demands of the international research enterprise as we move away from antiquated past practices.

Table 1: How to prepare students for this award—interested advisors and students should refer to the program Web site: http://oxcam.gpp.nih.gov.

Freshman year—Top students with interests in a science career should plan their collegiate curriculum to obtain a solid foundation in basic biology, chemistry, and mathematical sciences. Beginning in the second semester, they should seek opportunities for laboratory experience. Following first year, they can consider the Summer Intern Program (SIP) at NIH for summer employment for eight or more weeks with a stipend provided (see http://www.training.nih.gov/student/sip/). Some medical centers, research institutions, and universities have similar programs. Many foundations provide grant support for these summer opportunities.

Sophomore year—Students should try to develop an experience in one area or lab that interests them so they can gain in-depth exposure and independence in the laboratory.

Junior year—Students should begin preparing for the GRE or MCAT tests, which should be taken in the spring of the junior year or fall of the senior year. Students should also discuss their plans for a PhD or MD/PhD and their commitment to a biomedical research career with their advisors. Information will be provided to fellowship advisors so that students can participate in conference calls regarding the NIH/Oxford/Cambridge Scholars Program.

Senior year—Students should check the program Web site for the application deadline and complete the required GRE or MCAT. Students should discuss their applications with faculty members, especially those with whom they've worked in a research laboratory setting (this is more useful to their application than an evaluation by a professor who has instructed them in a didactic class). Three letters of recommendation are required. These should come from faculty members who are very familiar with the students' academic backgrounds and, importantly, from research mentors at both the university and from significant summer research experiences. A good option for students who would like to take a year or more off to solidify their credentials or commitment to biomedical research is to participate in the Postbaccalaureate Intramural Research Training Award and other programs in which they carry out research in a full-time, paid position in a research laboratory at the NIH (see http://www.training.nih.gov/student/). Rhodes, Marshall, and Churchill Scholars who are pursuing biomedical studies will be sent application materials to extend these scholarships with an NIH/Oxford/Cambridge Scholarship to a full PhD including work on the NIH campus. Students who have had their own research projects or have contributed physically and intellectually to collaborative projects are most competitive in this program. We welcome applications from students with engineering, mathematical, or physical science majors, but ask these students to elaborate on why they are interested in biomedical research and how their academic background has prepared them for this endeavor.

Medical Students—Students wishing to try out full-time research may be interested in the Howard Hughes Medical Institutes/NIH Research Scholars Program, based on the NIH campus (http://www.hhmi.org/cloister/). HHMI/NIH Scholars often extend their research as NIH/Oxford/Cambridge Scholars. Alternatively, medical students can apply directly to the NIH/Oxford/Cambridge Scholars Program. In both instances students can apply to be part of the NIH National MD-PhD Program. Students interested in the MD-PhD program should apply independently to the Medical Scientist Training Program (MSTP) at participating medical schools. Upon simultaneous acceptance to a medical school MSTP and the NIH/Oxford/Cambridge Scholars Program, the program directors will work with the medical schools to jointly administer the award.

5

Understanding the Odds
A Reader's Perspective

DOUG CUTCHINS

Doug Cutchins is the Director of Service and Social Commitment at Grinnell College and advises students on postgraduate service and scholarship opportunities. He administers the Grinnell Corps and oversees the Community Service Center. A 1993 graduate of Grinnell College, he majored in history and was certified to teach. Mr. Cutchins holds an MA in history from the University of Connecticut. He has taught social studies in urban and rural schools in Iowa and North Carolina and has served as a Peace Corps volunteer in Suriname from 1995–1997. He received the James Madison Fellowship and has served as a reader for that award. He has served on the boards of directors for the Iowa Peace Institute, for the Grinnell United Way (serving as president for two years), and for the National Association of Fellowships Advisors. He is a coauthor of the 8th and 9th editions of Volunteer Vacations, published by Chicago Review Press, with the 10th edition currently being prepared for publication.

The two files stared at us from the table. My reading partner and I had dissected each one of them thoroughly and had been through each multiple times. We knew the candidates—both women—as well as we could, given the papers that described them. We knew their grades from their first-year English classes, how they had spent their summers after the second year, how they spent their time outside of class, the impact they had each had on their campuses, and how much their peers and professors admired them. We knew all this.

And after three days sitting side by side in a small room, buttoned up with twelve other scholarship committee members from around the country, we knew each other as well as we now knew these two files. I knew that when my reading partner was annoyed with a file, she'd sigh before she would get up and go refill her water. She knew all about my annoying tendency to talk back to the candidates (out loud, no less) when they got overly preachy in their essays. We both knew what in a particular candidate would make the other person swoon and had reached a good-natured détente in our ability to compromise.

But all of that camaraderie had ended with this, our final pile of scholarship files to read, judge, and from which we would pick several winners. As usual we had little problem sifting out the candidates who—while good—were not going to be scholarship winners. And there were one or two who were so obviously stellar that our discussion was nothing more than a glowing recitation of the students' achievements. But now we were down to the hard work—the really hard work. We had one scholarship to go and two candidates who deserved it. I liked one of the candidates; my reading partner favored the other. We both saw the other's argument and agreed that both were deserving candidates. But we both knew who each of us wanted to win the prize, and there existed no Solomonic answer to our problem.

We had faced this situation in other batches of files. We had worked through our earlier difficulties with relative ease because one of us was always ready to give in and let the other prevail, knowing that next time the favor would be returned. Maybe it was just the fact that this time there was no next time. Maybe it was that we were both tired, ready to travel home to our families. Maybe I had talked back to a file one too many times. Or maybe it truly was that both of these candidates were incredibly well qualified, that both deserved this scholarship, and that neither of us wanted to admit that one student would walk away empty-handed, always wondering why her top-notch application had not been selected, never knowing that she was so close to winning and had a strong advocate on the committee.

After twenty minutes of this back-and-forth, we decided that we were never going to come to a solution. Neither of us would bend to the other's wisdom or even claim some sort of moral superiority by allowing the other to prevail. We returned the files to the chair of the scholarship committee and glumly told her that another team of two would have to reread these files (becoming the fifth and sixth pairs of eyes to go over the documents in this long weekend) and decide between them. We were disappointed that we had failed in our appointed duty, but relieved of the burden of our decision.

As we waited impatiently for the other team to come back with its verdict, I suddenly found myself wracked with a combination of worry, guilt, and uncertainty. How did I know that I was right? Why had I not been willing to compromise? Who was I to hold the other candidate at arm's length from winning a scholarship? Could I not trust my reading partner after the scores of files we had been through already? I danced lightly on the balls of my feet. Maybe I should change my mind. Maybe I should go over there and tell the chair of the committee that I was wrong. Would they pull that other reading team? Had I abdicated power, or could I still declare one student to be a scholarship winner?

Before I could move, the door from the porch opened, and the pair of readers returned. They agreed that it was a difficult choice—that these were two wonderful young women. Both deserved the scholarship. Both had a lot to commend them. And they did not want to choose, but if they had to, then they thought they guessed they would maybe go with the candidate I liked. We all exhaled.

I have had the opportunity to be a selection committee member for three well-known national scholarship or fellowship opportunities. Each provided a different look into the world of scholarship administration and decision making, and each taught me lessons that I have used when I returned to my day job as Grinnell College's scholarship advisor. For those who have taught, the experience is not dissimilar to the shift from the student's desk to the teacher's podium, and you suddenly realize what you should have done to be successful as a student. Having worked with foundations, read applications, and chosen the best from among them, I now have a much better sense of how to help my own candidates prepare their applications to go in front of a national committee.

As scholarship advisors, our work sometimes feels like that famous cartoon where two mathematicians stand in front of a chalkboard filled with complex computations and notations on the left side. There is a note toward the middle that says, "And then a miracle occurs," before the equation resolves itself as "= 1." Our own computations and notations are those long advising sessions with candidates, helping them not only to think about who they are, what they have done, where they are going, and how they are going to get there, but also how to articulate that in a way that makes sense to someone else. Then we toss the papers into an online application or FedEx, cross our fingers, and wait for the miracle to occur, hoping that this equation will also "= 1."

The good news is that the "then a miracle occurs" part of the process is actually a quite rational, rigorous, and planned selection of candidates. Foundations work incredibly hard to provide committee members with matrices, examples of stellar applications, samples to read and critique, and hours of reading and training before readers ever get to put eyes or a red pen on a real application. One foundation I worked with even had a PhD-level statistician on hand who constantly looked at the data we were generating and would circulate to tap reviewers on the shoulder who were five-tenths of a point too generous on this measurement, or those who needed to use the full range of scores on that scale. The dedication shown by foundation coordinators to getting the process right—to recruiting and choosing the best candidates to name as scholars—is admirable. Foundations care deeply about their mission, the selection process, and ultimately about their scholars.

Despite all of the foundations' best efforts, though, this is still a subjective, luck-filled process. Were it not, there would be no need for scholarship committee members; the foundations could just plug information into a computer, write algorithms, and have the scholarships decided by Excel. We may actually be getting closer to this point: one foundation representative told me that they had a computer programmer who successfully predicted 85 percent of the scholars out of last year's applicant pool, based on a few simple, objective metrics. But until the robots take over, we are left with selection processes that are devised by, run by, and decided by eminently fallible humans, full of their own foibles, faults, experiences, and preferences. After one selection process, my head swollen by the power that had recently been bestowed upon me by the foundation, I declared to a fellow committee member that I thought we, as a group, had done a stellar job in selecting a great group of scholars. He looked at me with the wisdom of many more years on this committee than I possessed and said that in his estimation, were we to erase all of our work and have a new committee arrive immediately and read all of the same files, they would select no more than 60 percent of the same candidates we had decided upon.

In addition to the subjective nature of scholarship selection, another reason for this disparity is that the majority of the applicants for these scholarships are unbelievably good, and getting better all the time. But here is the brutal truth that I learned from reading all of these files: being a really, really strong candidate for a national scholarship or fellowship makes an applicant no more than average. A student who meets or exceeds all of the standards, criteria, and eligibility measures for a given award is pretty thoroughly mid-pack. The sheer number of extraordinary candidates out there—students with high GPAs, leadership profiles, interesting extracurricular activities, strong letters of recommendation, earnest intentions, and brilliant plans for the future—can be overwhelming at times. And, of course, NAFA is not helping make committee members' jobs any easier: as we recruit more candidates, make them aware of opportunities to live their passions, and assist them in presenting the strongest applications possible, the overall quality of these pools continues to rise, which, in turn, means that NAFA members do even more to help their candidates try to stand out. Which raises the bar again, and the cycle continues.

So we are faced with a profession wherein we are constantly improving our best practices, always putting forward more and better-prepared candidates, and for zero-sum scholarship opportunities that are subjectively chosen and inherently luck filled. At the least, then, we have a positive obligation to ensure that we are recruiting the right candidates, preparing them properly, and helping them make the most of the process of applying for these awards. To this end it would be very helpful if all foundations were as open as possible with their selection models, processes, and criteria. Some scholarships already post their committee members' rating forms online, give examples of successful and nonsuccessful answers on application forms, and help candidates prepare for interviews (as applicable); but not nearly all of them do so, or do all of these things. I have spoken with a number of foundation representatives who closely guard their selection criteria about why they choose not to release that information. These conversations lead me to believe foundations do so based on the assumption that opening up selection processes will generate candidates who simply write their applications to meet these criteria and standards.

My experience suggests the opposite: that publishing how decisions are made, giving models for successful applications, and sharing advice on how to improve an application creates to two positive outcomes. First, students who may be an acceptable, but not great, fit for a particular scholarship recognize this early in the process and decide to seek alternate options for funding. Second, those who do continue on with an application are better able to provide the information the committee needs to make as informed a decision as possible. In any given application, the full picture of the candidate is not known to the committee member—there are life experiences, extracurricular activities, motivations, and beliefs that go unexpressed within the confines of the application form. Knowing which of these experiences to include and which to exclude is a difficult task for students and for those of us who advise them; more direction, openness, and advice from foundations will help candidates present themselves more effectively and accurately.

After the pair of readers returned to the conference room, having selected the candidate that I favored out of the two my reading partner and I had been hopelessly deadlocked over, all of us stood around awkwardly and somewhat painfully. How did we know we had made the right choice? What if I had given in to my reading partner earlier and her favored candidate had won? It seemed strange that these two candidates had no idea how close each of them had been to the other's fate—and never would. What if this scholarship opened doors for one that would remain closed to the other? Was it really fair for us to make such a subjective decision about two candidates so similarly qualified? But what choice did we have?

As we stood there trying to puzzle out the answers to these questions, the door opened again and another team of two readers entered the room. Looking at the two of them was like a mirror for my reading partner and me fifteen minutes earlier—tired, frustrated, and unsure of how to proceed. We all steeled ourselves for another tie that would have to be broken.

Their problem was different. Yes, they were also down to their final two. Yes, they also could not decide between these two. But their discussions had taken a different turn, as they eventually realized that neither of these two candidates was up to the caliber of the rest of the scholars they had selected over the course of the last few days. Would it be acceptable, they wondered, if they declined to award a scholarship to either of these candidates? What might happen to the unused funds in that case?

The committee chair knew exactly what to do. She took the funds that would have gone to one of those two candidates and gave it to the nonselected student in our pairing. Thanks to a fair, caring, dedicated foundation, some hard-working committee members, and a subjective yet open scholarship selection process, both of the two candidates my reading partner and I had ached and argued over would now be named scholars.

Scholarship advisors are always preaching the value of the application process to our candidates, and rightly so. But we all also need to take solace from and know that the "then a miracle occurs" moment that happens is important for all of us to understand better.

6

Creating Opportunities for Experiential Education in a Resource-Strained Environment[1]

PAULA WARRICK

Paula Warrick joined the career center at American University in 1999 as the Director of the Office of Merit Awards and has worked with successful scholarship applicants for an array of study abroad grants, tuition scholarships, and prestigious internships. She has seen the application process from multiple sides, having both mentored students and applied for fellowships herself. Dr. Warrick won her first nationally competitive scholarship as a high school senior and went on to receive a lecturing fellowship from the National Gallery of Art in Washington and a dissertation fellowship from the Samuel H. Kress Foundation in New York. She is a firm believer in the rewards of the application process, including the chance to develop more realistic career goals and close relationships with faculty. She is also an adjunct professor of Liberal Studies at Georgetown University. Before coming to American, she taught Art History at the University of Kentucky, the University of Virginia, and Rice University. Paula Warrick currently serves as the President of the National Association of Fellowships Advisors (NAFA).

You Can't Squeeze Blood from a Turnip" was my sister's suggested title for my advice piece on how to grow experiential education initiatives on campuses that lack an infrastructure to support them. In her mind a lack of resources is almost always an insurmountable obstacle, and I was foolish for volunteering to write an essay on an impractical topic. Her pragmatism was honed through years of work responding to constituent requests on behalf of a U.S. senator.

The only possible response, from my standpoint as a history major and an older sibling, was to research my sister's cliché. Perhaps I could unearth some hidden meaning that she had not intended when she teased me. Maybe it was possible to create something out of—seemingly—nothing.

An initial search taught me that most sources do paraphrase the expression roughly as, "You can't pry something out of someone if they don't have it to give away in the first place" (my sister's implied meaning). The *New Dictionary of Cultural Literacy*, however, offered a ray of hope with its definition: "You can only get from people what they are willing to give." In this sense my sister's title does not close off the possibility of offering further advice. What people have to give away is non-negotiable, but what they are willing to give may be susceptible to persuasion.

In the spirit of this second definition, I would like to propose a process to help scholarship advisors to advocate for support for applied learning on campuses that are under-resourced in this area. In my mind the best way to build support for experiential learning activities, such as service learning and credit-bearing internships, is to work from the inside of the institution outward. Begin by searching inside your college or university for allies, and then, if your resources still seem limited, seek help externally. The process I envision has six steps.

Step 1: Refine your understanding of experiential learning. Review model syllabi to get a feel for different ways of integrating experiential learning into college-level courses. Campus Compact (http://www.compact.org), a coalition of college and university presidents committed to service learning, has posted syllabi in dozens of academic subjects on its Web site. You can supplement this knowledge with information gleaned from any academic regulations your institution has established to govern service learning or internships for credit. Such guidelines can help you to deepen your awareness of factors that determine whether an experiential learning activity is academically substantive. If your institution lacks such guidelines, review those developed by other institutions.[2]

Step 2: Take stock of what you have. You might next assess whether and to what extent your campus truly *is* under-resourced in the area of service learning. A series of questions can help you to make this determination:

- *Campus expertise.* Does your campus have a community service center, and if so, how many staff members work there? Where is the office housed? An office located in the "campus life" division may lack the academic respectability of one whose director reports to a provost or academic dean.
- *Faculty buy-in and support.* Do deans and department chairs appear to understand and find value in experiential education? You might explore whether mentoring students in academic internships and service-learning projects carries weight in the merit review process for faculty. Support for faculty involvement in service learning, in the form of teaching workshops, curriculum development grants, and sabbaticals for service-learning research, may indicate respect for experiential learning in the upper echelons of administration.
- *Student recognition.* Are internships and service-learning activities documented on students' transcripts? How many credit hours can be earned and do students receive a letter grade for their efforts?

Step 3: Familiarize yourself with potential obstacles to building support for experiential education on campus (why, not what, people are unwilling to give). A lack of resources for experiential education programming at your institution may mean more than inadequate funding. If your campus does not have a long history of promoting experiential education, you may have to advocate for its respectability. If internships and service learning are to be fully linked to students' curricula, and if students are to receive academic credit for such activities, faculty involvement is essential. Inadequate compensation or no tradition of faculty incentives for such activities can impede faculty participation. Even professors who are compensated through stipends, course releases, or additional support in the tenure and promotion process may lack the pedagogical foundation needed to integrate service learning or internships for credit into their teaching. Offices that attempt to offer guidance on this front must work carefully in order to avoid giving the impression that they want, as one of my faculty colleagues put it, to "teach my class for me."

Finally, the main beneficiaries of experiential learning—students themselves—may not have arrived at college with a mature sense of what can be gained from these educational experiences. Once they have completed a well-crafted internship or become involved in community-based research, though, they may become powerful advocates of your efforts to improve the climate for experiential education on campus.

Step 4: Search for internal and local resources. Even if you conclude that there is no campus-wide support for experiential education, you may discover hidden resources in the form of faculty colleagues who are working independently to integrate service learning into their courses. I conducted information interviews with various administrators in offices across my campus and learned that one of our photography professors gives her students the option of creating a final project for additional service-learning credit. Participants work with local nonprofit organizations to understand and document an important social issue facing Washington, DC. The creative work they generate, on topics ranging from immigration to animal rights, must be offered to the project sponsor for use as an advocacy tool. Another colleague in our school of education developed a service-learning component for a youth summit series developed by local education and arts nonprofits. He trained sixteen college students to serve as field observers for the summits and worked with them to transform their individual data into a group report. Through this project the participants supported the overall aim of the summits: to ensure that local school children had a voice in major school reforms to be undertaken in compliance with the No Child Left Behind Act.[3] Your center for teaching excellence may be able to help you to identify colleagues like these, who support experiential education and are willing to help promote such activities on campus.

In addition to building a network of faculty support, you might ask your center for teaching excellence to offer workshops on how to design class projects with out-of-classroom experiences in mind. If you live in an urban area, you may also have access to special community resources designed to build institutional capacity to support experiential education. Washington is home to the CoRAL (Community Research and Learning) Network (http://www.coralnetwork.org), a consortium of local colleges, universities, and local nonprofit organizations that promotes civic engagement among undergraduates. The consortium selects fifteen faculty fellows each spring, who work collectively to deepen their understanding of service learning and to share strategies for incorporating it into their teaching.

Step 5: Create your own resources for students, drawing on external support if need be.

You might broaden your Web site to include information on the benefits of experiential education and opportunities for students in this area. Through the Internet you might:

- Provide information on formal opportunities for students to get involved in service learning through your college or university. Does your institution offer a credit option for service learning or internships, for instance? If so, explain how this works and what benefits it provides.
- Create blogs to have students talk about the out-of-classroom experiences they have pursued and how they have shaped their overall academic interests and plans.
- Offer links to resources that can help students find ways to become involved in experiential education. Thoughts on types of resources you might include appear in the appendix to this chapter.

Step 6: Evaluate. Once you have successfully involved your students in experiential learning activities, talk to them about their experiences. Students should return to campus feeling as if they spent the semester or summer helping an organization to fulfill its core mission, rather than performing busywork. If the experience is well designed, the service learning provider will have conveyed respect for the student's participation and demonstrated a thoughtful understanding of what it stood to gain by involving undergraduates in its work, and so we come to a second kind of "turnip." Assuming that the sponsoring organization is not crippled by a lack of resources, its own constraints in terms of time, money, and personnel may be an impetus to develop meaningful service-learning opportunities for undergraduates. Community organizers and employers may feel like they have their own turnips to squeeze, and this may in turn determine what they are willing to give to the talented students we send their way.

Selected Online Resources on Experiential Education[4]

SAMPLE SYLLABI AND OTHER RESOURCES

- *American University Career Center* (http://www.american.edu/careercenter) has a good deal of information on student internships for credit, including student blogs and podcasts, academic regulations about internships, and advice to faculty on how to integrate an internship into an academic curriculum. Check the resource sections for faculty and for students.
- *Campus Compact* (http://www.compact.org) is a coalition of college and university presidents committed to experiential education. It publishes newsletters, has an online bookstore, and posts model syllabi with service-learning components.
- *CoRAL (Community Research and Learning) Network* (http://www.coralnetwork.org) offers links to academic journals that publish articles on service-learning and community-based research. This organization also awards fellowships to faculty members in the Washington metropolitan area who wish to incorporate service learning into their teaching.
- *National Association of Colleges and Employers* (http://www.naceweb.org) requires a password to access much of the information it provides on internships for credit, which your career center may be able to provide.
- *The National Society for Experiential Education* (http://www.NSEE.org) disseminates information on research and best practices in the field of experiential education, in part through publications available through its online bookstore.

OPPORTUNITIES FOR CAPACITY-BUILDING AT THE CAMPUS LEVEL

- *The Corella and Bertram F. Bonner Foundation* (http://www.bonner.org) provides college-age students with financial and academic support to engage in service learning. To qualify, students must attend an institution designated as a Bonner Leaders Program Campus (there are more than fifty BLP campuses to date, and nonmember institutions may apply to become one). The foundation maintains links with national and international organizations that offer internships and volunteer opportunities. It also distributes training materials, hosts national conferences, and grants AmeriCorps education awards to students on participating campuses.

- *Learn and Serve America* (http://www.learnandserve.gov) is the service-learning arm of the Corporation for National and Community Service. In order to facilitate capacity-building for service learning on campuses across the country, it offers individual and consortia grants to universities.

SUPPORT FOR STUDENTS—FELLOWSHIPS AND TECHNICAL ASSISTANCE

- *Everett Public Service Internship* (http://www.everettinternships.org) encourages students to explore public service careers by providing a paid summer internship in Washington, DC, or New York. Recipients earn $280/week for ten weeks and take part in various educational and social events. Participating organizations, which range from the Brooklyn Children's Museum to Human Rights Watch, agree to provide substantive internships as a condition of their involvement with the Everett program.
- *Roots and Shoots* (http://www.rootsandshoots.org) is associated with the Jane Goodall Institute and helps students to design or implement a service-learning project in the areas of the environment, animal welfare, and human rights. It also maintains lists of groups seeking new members for service-learning projects in various areas of the country. Roots and Shoots has a college programs office based in Arlington, Virginia.
- *The Building Bridges Coalition* (www.idealist.org/en/org/ 164194-332) lists organizations that specialize in placing volunteers overseas, and students can sign up to receive e-mail alerts on opportunities that match their volunteer profile. The coalition is associated with the Brookings Institution Initiative on International Volunteering and Service (www.brookings.edu/projects/volunteering.aspx). Brookings has proposed the creation of 10,000 congressionally-funded Global Service Fellowships as part of its initiative to double the number of American volunteers abroad by 2010. If created, the awards will be open to college students.

INTERNSHIP OPTIONS (UNPAID OR TUITION PAYMENT REQUIRED)

- *The Carter Center, Atlanta, Georgia* (http://www.cartercenter.org/) is a nongovernmental organization founded by Jimmy and Rosalynn Carter. It focuses on a range of human-centered issues including human rights, public health, and world hunger. Internships are unpaid but substantive, which means in this case that no more than 30 percent of a student's time will be devoted to administrative work. Students may receive academic credit for their internships, provided they have arranged for a supervisor at their home institution at the time of application. Some need-based financial assistance is available to program participants. The center also has a Graduate Assistantship Program that pays $3,500/week for ten weeks of full-time work.
- *The Washington Center for Internships and Academic Seminars, Washington, DC* (http://www.twc.edu/) is a nonprofit organization that specializes in providing college students with internships in Washington, DC, for academic credit.
- *The Washington Semester Program, Washington, DC* (http://www.american.edu/washingtonsemester) at American University provides an eight-credit seminar, a four-credit internship in Washington, and a three-credit internship or independent research project. Credits transfer automatically for students who attend one of two hundred WSP member institutions. The program is open to students who attend nonmember colleges and universities.

7

A Newcomer's Guide to Scholarship Advising

CAROL SHINER WILSON

Carol Shiner Wilson has served as Dean of the College for Academic Life at Muhlenberg College for thirteen years. She earned a BA in French from Cornell College, an MA in French from the University of Missouri, an MA in English from the University of Kansas, and a PhD in English from Indiana University in 1985. She has taught French, English, and Women's Studies at the North Shore Country Day School (Winnetka, IL), Lafayette College, and Muhlenberg College. She has published books and articles about British women writers and cochaired Muhlenberg's Middle States reaccreditation steering committee for the 2006 review. In 1998 she created the Postgraduate Awards Initiative at Muhlenberg and has been a member of NAFA since its inception.

The number of institutions committing resources to advising for nationally competitive scholarships has exploded over the last decade. New advisors, whether in newly created positions or in positions already designated by the institution, face a variety of both opportunities and challenges. How does a new advisor navigate the waters? How does he or she determine the shoals? What is the destination? What are the implications of ever-increasing resources committed to scholarship advising while the number of scholarships is not expanding significantly? What resources are at hand for the newcomer? Over 100 professionals self-identifying as new in the field signed up for NAFA's 2007 Boot Camp, a preconference workshop at the national conference in Washington, DC. Although the phrase *boot camp* calls up images of shaved heads, shouting drill sergeants, and twenty-mile hikes in full gear, the NAFA Boot Camp was a kinder, gentler sort. Yet boot camps, whether connected to the army, navy, or scholarship advising, are intense introductions for the newcomer to the institution in question and to its broader culture.

Campus Culture

For any new professional in an academic setting, it is vital to understand and connect to the culture of the place. There are multiple constituencies: faculty, administration, students, and alumni or friends of the college. Check out key sites and make sure the connections between the fellowships office and what the institution says about itself are consistent. For example, admissions offices often craft a compelling story in order to attract students. What is that narrative? At Muhlenberg College, for example, that narrative stresses small classes, close working relationships with faculty, and interactive pedagogy, which is consistent with the dedication of college faculty, who spend many hours with students outside the classroom, laboratory, and studio. Some of those hours are involved in close work with students who wish to apply for prestigious awards.

At several institutions the admissions offices stress the number of prize winners there are among the faculty—Nobel Laureates, MacArthurs, NSFs, and so forth—so the connection to student winners of prestigious awards is an easy one. Any institution seeking intellectually gifted students will be happy to advertise programs assisting students who are applying for nationally competitive scholarships. Many institutions include in their mission statements the value of civic engagement. For such institutions the connection between a Truman or Rotary Scholarship and the institution's mission is easily demonstrable.

Most institutions regularly undergo self-scrutiny and strategic planning. It is important to identify the connections between the work the fellowships advisor does and the college's strategic plan. At Muhlenberg, for example, the connection between prestigious awards and the increased support for student research is clear. My office oversees competition for in-house summer research grants in all disciplines and coordinates information for all undergraduate research, including faculty grants through NIH and NSF that fund student researchers. The development office is another important connection to make. Alumni are proud to say that students and recent graduates have been successful in competition for Fulbrights, Javits, and Trumans. Moreover, development offices find it valuable to be able to add those successes in grant applications to foundations. Certainly, making the connection between academics and the qualities of successful scholarship applicants is key in any institution. Although students are not incidental in this process, they do not set the agenda.

Advisors are most effective in their important work with students when they understand and connect to core components of the culture of the faculty and administration. Being visible is important, and the work must be seen as integral to the institution's culture. Sometimes the subcultures may seem contradictory, but demonstrating how the university's primary interests are served by effective work in the scholarships office is vital. It is, of course, also important to be knowledgeable about the particular scholarships and how they connect to individual interests. At Muhlenberg, for example, I do targeted marketing to our honors advisors and students and to professors in a variety of disciplines from literature to public health. I have spoken in department meetings and at meetings of academic department heads and the Dean of Students staff.

An important dimension of a scholarship advisor's job is to educate the community, and that is particularly evident when it comes to what "success" means. As I have said on many occasions to constituents inside and outside my institution, the scholarship process is not about notches on a belt. Though a list of students who have won awards or placed as finalists in competitions for Javits, British Marshalls, Fulbrights, and more is significant, the very real work and reward is in the *process.* In my report to the Board of Trustees, for example, I talk about the process at the college and the close work we do with students as we help them pull together the components of their education, inside and outside the classroom, and think about themselves and their futures in a more intentional way through the scholarship process. That process may begin as early as the first year, when many students are just beginning to explore their values, skills, and interests. Celebrating those who win or receive honorable mentions in awards encourages other students to engage, but it is also helpful to tell stories about the appreciation students have for the process and its value, and to share "alternative" success stories.

At Muhlenberg, for example, I tell two such stories. One is about a student who claimed that she would not have gotten into a PhD program in public policy at Princeton had she not gone through the careful process of self-reflection and multiple drafts in applying for a Jack Kent Cooke (that she did not receive). Another is about a woman who claimed the same for her admission with full funding to the history PhD program of her choice after applying for a Javits.

Campus Context

Related to campus culture, the context includes particulars such as reporting structures, budgets, and processes for gathering information about candidates and academic departments. Surveys of NAFA members indicate that most fellowship offices are housed in academic affairs and that many current, seasoned advisors held academic positions, including teaching, prior to taking up scholarship advising. The models are multiple and at times idiosyncratic, depending in part upon the longevity of the service, how it has been defined and grown, and the personnel involved. Job titles vary widely and include Director of Undergraduate Research and Fellowship Advising; Associate Director for Fellowships, Scholarships, and Graduate School Advising; Associate Director of the University Honors Program; Director, Pre-Health and National Awards Advising Office; Dean of the College for Academic Life; Associate Dean of the College; Associate Provost; and, among the most unusual, Director of Social Commitment. A few programs are housed in student affairs, typically in a career services office, and representative titles are Coordinator of Career Services and Assistant Director of Career Services. As titles indicate, many advisors have multiple responsibilities, although reports indicate that the prestigious scholarship advising is the most time-consuming.

Regardless of where the office is housed, the visible connection of the office and the director with the academic mission is essential. Regardless of the site and level of responsibility, it is also important that the service have an adequate budget over which the director or dean has direct control with access to funding for special events such as the college or university president's reception or a dinner honoring students and faculty who have participated in the awards process. Academic institutions are by necessity collaborative ventures. Having a plan of action is vital, and that plan should include whom to access and how. For example, at Pomona College, Paula Goldsmid works closely with the registrar in order to get a list of high-achieving (by GPA) students, their advisors, and contact information in order to make appropriate and specific contacts. And there are others who can assist with identification of potential candidates and dissemination of information as well, including honors program advisors, community service directors, and coaches.

Faculty members are always critical partners in this enterprise, and developing a plan to connect with professors who know students well and will be willing to identify and partner with the fellowships office in working with students is vital. Faculty must believe in the advisor's own understanding of and commitment to the academic enterprise. Many scholarship advisors will make sure to send letters noting faculty participation in the program to department heads or chief academic officers. Several of us are asked annually to provide letters on faculty service for their tenure or promotion files. Karna Walter includes more on the importance of faculty's contribution to the scholarship effort in Chapter 10, "Involving Faculty in the Scholarship Effort."

Student Recruitment

According to Lisa Grimes, the College of William and Mary uses a "cradle to the grave" approach in recruiting candidates for competitive awards: first-year students through alumni. It is important not to overlook alumni, because at times undergraduates do not know their goals or may in other ways not yet be ready to apply for scholarships until one or more years after graduation. Professors are crucial for identifying potential candidates, and William and Mary has, as do most programs, a campus faculty committee that reads applications and makes recommendations for nationally competitive awards. Food is a motivator on virtually any campus. Students are inclined to come to informational meetings where refreshments are served; feeding faculty during endorsement committee meetings proves valuable; and having a reception or dinner in recognition of students and faculty is an important touch.

With information coming in at different times from different sources about many students, having a reliable tracking system is critical. William and Mary uses a questionnaire, which can be sorted by many categories, including alphabetically and by school year. To facilitate communication, the office maintains this group on a school Listserv. The college also has a separate faculty Listserv. Drawing on student support, the office uses student advisors who assist with basic advising and with practice interviews.

Nuts and Bolts

New advisors, whether new to the campus or not, need to connect with anyone previously involved with awards advising. Meeting with faculty and staff will give the new advisor an understanding of the culture and previous practices and may help the new advisor to anticipate land mines. Experienced or new, any advisor will find NAFA a resource-rich organization. From the volunteer mentoring program to a large collection of practical documents relating to various aspects of the awards process, NAFA offers new advisors a convenient and extensive network of support.[1]

As Laura Damuth, University of Nebraska-Lincoln, and Jim Duban, University of North Texas, note, fellowships advisors need to be clear and consistent in explaining the selection criteria set forth by foundations, the campus process for students and faculty involved in the competition, and internal deadlines connected to the campus process. Materials, both written and electronic, should be engaging and easy to negotiate. Materials and advice in person should also be made readily available and should include information about the elements of effective personal statements required in all applications as well as how to approach faculty to request letters of recommendation. Although campus approaches vary, most will have a combination of workshops on writing personal statements and will provide assistance from faculty or staff as the applicants work through multiple drafts.

Developing a network of knowledgeable faculty to evaluate applications and conduct practice interviews is essential. Depending upon the campus culture, a credit-bearing course in which students go through the steps of self-exploration, identification of appropriate awards, and the writing of applications might be appropriate. Jim Duban teaches such a course at the University of North Texas. On other campuses an issues-oriented course to stimulate thinking might be warranted. On many others, any inkling of a credit-bearing course that would presume to supplant the work done by the faculty would be unacceptable. Some foundations have also voiced concern about scholarship preparation courses.

Whether or not a student receives an award, the student should be celebrated for having participated in the process. A great many institutions have special lunches, dinners, or receptions at the end of the academic year to congratulate students and faculty who have participated. These events are usually hosted by the president of the institution and often afford any student the opportunity to make remarks about the process.

Perspective

Fellowships advising is challenging, but it is also rewarding. Ultimately advisors are generous folk, dedicated to the students, their growth, and their success. It takes collaboration across the campus with others who share a passion for the students and for learning. If the numbers seem discouraging, or that "big award" seems elusive, always step back and remember that we are in this because of the students. Every advisor has stories of special students who made it worthwhile and whose worlds were changed because we and our colleagues have cared enough to listen and to guide. Keep in mind and remind others what this is about—students.[2-3]

8

Encouraged to Apply
Diversity and the Scholarship Process

LISA J. KNEPSHIELD

Lisa Knepshield is the Fellowship Coordinator for the Graduate College of the University of Illinois at Chicago. Prior to becoming a fellowship advisor, Lisa worked in the field of international education for ten years. She worked in the Institute of International Education in New York and Chicago, primarily with the Fulbright program, including international Fulbright Scholars, U.S. applicants, and national screening committees. She then became Assistant Director of the Office of International Services at University of Illinois at Chicago, working with international faculty. Since becoming a fellowship advisor, she has turned her research interest to minority applicants for fellowships for graduate study.

"Women and students from underrepresented minority groups are especially encouraged to apply." How many fellowship and scholarship
applications end with that gentle, but firm, remonstrance? In recent years
many if not most award applications now include such a suggestion, which
fellowship advisors take to heart. Discussions on ways to recruit students for
major awards, particularly those students who have not traditionally received
them, have occurred since NAFA's founding. Fellowships advisors across the
country work actively with admissions offices and other campus resources to
identify, contact, and encourage underrepresented students. Advisors, like
other campus administrators, know well the importance of having a diverse
applicant pool. And yet, despite these efforts, fellowship agencies are often
dissatisfied with a general lack of nontraditional applicants.

Two questions immediately emerge. How do we address this? And,
what tools can we develop to analyze existing data and assess national
trends that might provide insight into the problem? The first question is
much more practically answered. The second question, as theoretical and
hard to answer as it is, also warrants discussion.

Experiences in recruiting and advising underrepresented students are
as different as the universities that NAFA represents. Looking at four specific institutions—the University of Maryland at Baltimore County, the
University of Rochester, Union College, and the University of Illinois at
Chicago—provides some insight into issues of engaging diverse groups in
the fellowship process. No institution can be considered absolutely representative, but these four include a large public university, a small private
university, a small liberal arts college, and finally an urban state institution. Although each type of institution faces different obstacles, the strategies that advisors have developed at each of these institutions are worth
considering when establishing a fellowships office diversity initiative.

The University of Maryland at Baltimore County

MULTIPLE RESOURCES

The University of Maryland at Baltimore County, part of the whole university system of Maryland, is a fair size: about 9,500 undergraduates and
2,500 graduate students. About 37 percent of those students are defined as
minorities. Presumably, in order to increase the pool of diverse students,

that's where one starts. If the number of students a fellowships advisor sees directly mirrors the student population (which it does not, of course; but for the sake of argument), then fewer than four of every ten students will be from an underrepresented group. Once other variables come into play, such as the students' majors, achievements, outside interests, volunteer activities, career interests, and so forth, the pool becomes less and less diverse.

So what strategies has the University of Maryland at Baltimore County developed to overcome the decline in numbers? First, it defines itself as an honors university, so all students from a variety of backgrounds have a higher-than-average level of achievement. This is quite different from many institutions represented in NAFA, whose members are affiliated with honors colleges and who often restrict their work to a small percentage of the student body.

Though it is an honors university, the institution also houses an Honors College, but the University of Maryland at Baltimore County structurally separates the Honors College and the Prestigious Scholarships Advising Office (Nancy Miller, former director). Within this office, time and resources are directed toward recruiting and advising minority students from the entire student body, not just those in the Honors College. By separating the two offices, there is less chance that the same group of students will be repeatedly contacted about various opportunities or that the university structure itself will limit certain types of outreach.

Although the institutional structure of the University of Maryland at Baltimore County works to its campus's fellowships advising office's advantage, it might not work as effectively at every institution. Many advising offices, tied to career offices, research programs, or honors offices, report that the connection is a positive one, citing a mutual benefit of such combinations in a one-stop advising approach. Even if a director would like the office to be a separate entity, few advisors around the country have enough influence on their own campuses to make it happen.

The University of Rochester

INSTITUTIONAL COMMITMENT

In contrast to the University of Maryland at Baltimore County, the University of Rochester has about half the number of undergraduates and a slightly larger number of graduate students (2,900). Major fellowships advising comes out of the Center for Academic Support, which includes a number of offices (Academic Services Office, Academic Records Office, and Academic Advising Office) that provide the Director of Fellowships (Belinda Redden) with needed resources.

In terms of diversity, institutional support is evident and far-reaching, to the point that its commitment to diversity is on the university's main homepage. In fact, not only is the university committed to diversifying the student body, but in 2006–2007 it also launched a faculty diversity campaign, described in detail in the university's annual report.[1] Although the report admits a lack of diversity within its faculty, the fact that the institution now supports a comprehensive effort toward improving faculty diversity works to the fellowships advisor's advantage in recruitment, on committees, and in application preparation. The positive effects of having a diverse faculty will be discussed again when we look at the University of Illinois at Chicago.

Like most fellowships advisors, the Director of Fellowships at Rochester works with the admissions office and other student services to identify an appropriate population of students, then organizes a series of information sessions, advising appointments, and other activities. Outreach efforts consume a large percentage of any advisor's time. Given this institution's explicit commitment to diversity, the director could spend a large percentage of her time just on underrepresented student recruitment.

In short the University of Rochester is not without resources. The essential problem—and this is shared by many smaller institutions across the country—is not a lack of staff support, but rather a lack of students. Although the institution as a whole is committed to a diverse pool of students, only a very limited number of students have the specific interests, the required grade point averages, and the leadership and volunteer activities that make them competitive fellowship applicants. Though the director certainly wants these students to be aware of the opportunities they have, there is a real concern that these few students will begin to feel pressured, even bombarded, by the number of fellowships and scholarships available to them and that they are encouraged to apply for.

No advisor wants to pressure applicants, particularly into applying for awards that students are not convinced they would even want to accept, simply to increase the number of underrepresented applicants. Nonetheless, working as realistically as we can with students does not decrease the perceived pressure from fellowship and scholarship foundations calling for a more diverse applicant pool. The only real solution in this case is long-term, involving each institution's commitment to diversity. These efforts should eventually yield a more diverse pool of students eligible for prestigious awards.

Union College

ALUMNI MENTORING

Union College is an undergraduate liberal arts college in Schenectady, New York. Although it offers more than forty majors, it lacks diversity in its student body. Currently 300 undergraduates are students of color.[2] Like most institutions in the same situation, it has developed a comprehensive effort to address the lack of diversity in the student population.

However, as Director of Post-Graduate Fellowships, Maggie Tongue has found that the effort to increase the diversity of the student body—and consequently that of the fellowship applicant pool—has actually had a detrimental effect. New admissions criteria can sometimes run against recruitment efforts for students who qualify for major fellowships. Specifically, many underrepresented students who qualify for major fellowships choose to attend other colleges, which are larger or more well-known. Many smaller, private liberal arts colleges find themselves in the same position as Union. Without lowering their considerably high academic standards, these colleges sometimes find themselves admitting underrepresented students who do not have comparable academic, activity, and volunteer résumés. Advising students for major fellowships who have great talent but who may not have had strong mentoring requires early identification of prospective applicants and a great deal of encouragement.

To do this the director relies heavily on Union alumni who have won major awards. Fortunately, fellowships advising is entering a phase for underrepresented students that includes a greater number of diverse alumni who have previously won nationally competitive awards. They are generally eager to help recruit and advise students on the process. Alumni mentoring is arguably the most successful strategy for recruiting and advising students from underrepresented groups. Advisors can provide all sorts of information sessions, but they are no substitute for the power of a role model. Seeing a Fulbright, Goldwater, Truman, or Rhodes Scholar of color or a woman NSF Graduate Research Fellow in a male-dominated discipline speaks volumes to the applicant.

Although each institution has its own strengths and obstacles, many of these are shared across our institutions: the ability to share resources with other offices on campus to identify qualified students, a lack of general diversity of the student body corresponding to a lack of diversity in fellowship applicants, institutional commitment to diversity in response to that lack, and proven outreach strategies involving peer and alumni mentoring.

The University of Illinois at Chicago

GETTING IT ALL INTO PERSPECTIVE

Before taking our summary of strategies and moving forward to more theoretical questions, let's look at a fourth institution. The University of Illinois at Chicago is one of a handful of public urban universities, centrally located in the nation's third-largest city. Like the city surrounding it, the undergraduate, graduate, and professional student bodies are some of the most diverse of all public universities in the United States—although, it must be noted, this is not entirely because of its location.[3] At the graduate and professional levels, many students are from out of state (including the international student population, which makes up about a quarter of all students on campus). The University of Illinois at Chicago's commitment to diversity, both within itself and as part of the University of Illinois system, is regularly described in various mission statements, affirmative action messages, and other public announcements.

Added to this, the University of Illinois at Chicago has one of most diverse faculty and staff rosters of U.S. public institutions. As mentioned in the discussion of the University of Rochester's faculty diversity study, the advantages of campus diversity are cyclical: a diverse faculty attracts a more diverse student body, and in turn those students earn degrees in larger numbers, such that a larger number of minority graduates become faculty; they in turn attract more minority students, and on it goes. In practical terms it is relatively easy for both Beth Powers, Director of the Office of Special Scholarship Programs (for undergraduate and professional students), and for me, Fellowship Coordinator for the Graduate College (for graduate students), to convene diverse campus review committees. Recruiting and advising underrepresented students becomes that much easier when an advisor can include diverse faculty committee members in addition to the mentoring provided by successful peers and alumni.

Within the Graduate College, the University of Illinois at Chicago offers a number of fellowships for students from underrepresented groups, and works with a state graduate fellowship program specifically devoted to diversifying faculty in Illinois. In day-to-day advising, I practically have a preselected group of committed graduate students who qualify for major awards. Although these students walk into my office at first to discuss the University of Illinois at Chicago's internal fellowships, like any advisor I make sure they have as much information as possible about major awards.

At the University of Illinois at Chicago, we have an explicit institutional commitment to diversity, a diverse student body at all levels, a diverse faculty and staff, two advising offices, and a very highly experienced fellowship director.[4] Even with all these advantages and resources available at our institution, we still have trouble recruiting minority students for major fellowships. That this is true should put the problem in perspective for both fellowships advisors and fellowship foundations.

We represent so many different institutions. We work with different university structures, mandates, and student populations, but we all face the same problem. This shared dilemma leads me to believe that there must be some general, national trends that we should be able to consult. Information abounds, but a comprehensive and comprehensible interpretation of data does not.

The National Science Foundation is assiduous in collecting and publishing statistics on all of the students who apply for its awards.[5] Likewise, the Javits administrators keep such data for the Department of Education;[6] IIE keeps statistics on the Fulbright applicant pool to share with the Department of State.[7] Research like this is the reason such agencies have come back to us as fellowships advisors for a more diverse applicant pool. Fellowship agencies are measuring the diversity of their various applicant pools, comparing them to the diversity of undergraduate, graduate, and professional students, and finding that those ratios do not match.

Again the numbers point to a problem, but the explanation of that problem is needed in order to address it. There are a few publications that describe the enormous changes in student demographics at all levels in the past ten years, in terms of gender, ethnicity, socioeconomic status, and more. For example, although it deals exclusively with graduate students (and doctoral students in particular), one of the reference works I find myself using repeatedly is Michael Nettles and Catherine Millett's *Three Magic Letters: Getting to PhD.*[8] Because their study is based on a very sophisticated survey instrument, and since they look quite specifically at ways graduate students fund their education, I have found it germane to my own work in advising graduate students in finding funding and applying for fellowships.

In order to meet the mandate of providing a more diverse applicant pool, we need tools. We understand the importance of outreach, maximizing campus resources, institutional commitment, and peer/alumni mentoring. In addition we know that applicant statistics from each major fellowship agency exist; we know that statistics on the student and faculty diversity of our own campuses exist; and we know that statistics on general undergraduate, graduate, and professional student bodies nationwide exist. How do we advance with what we know?

Those statistics need to be put together and analyzed in as many ways as we can find useful. This would be an enormous and ongoing task. Fellowships advisors, fellowship sponsors, and even outside agencies such as the Educational Testing Service, the Council of Graduate Schools, the American Association of Collegiate Registrars, and others would surely find such analyses as important and relevant to their work as we would find it to ours. The theme for the 2007 national NAFA conference in Washington, DC, was "Scholarships in a National Context." To recruit and advise underrepresented students successfully, we need to *see* that national context: we need analytical tools, themselves using existing statistics, to show us how we may improve. We must keep the necessity of these analytical tools squarely in mind as we grow as an organization.

9

Preparing for the Interview
Advice from a Gates Cambridge Scholar and Fellowships Advisor

LANCE OWEN

Lance Owen, the Associate Director of the Office of Nationally Competitive Awards, attended the University of Arkansas on a Sturgis Fellowship and completed his Bachelor of Arts in Music in May 2006. During his junior year, he studied abroad at the University of Cambridge, where he returned to complete an MPhil in Musicology on a Gates Cambridge Scholarship in 2007. After graduation Mr. Owen began work with nationally competitive and state scholarship advising, with Honors College events, and with recruitment efforts. He also serves as the Associate Director of the annual College Board Approved University of Arkansas Advanced Placement Summer Institute that hosts more than 300 teachers from across the country each year. He will begin a two-year commitment to Teach for America in the fall of 2009.

In August 2005, I joined a number of my friends in relinquishing the social opportunities of the first weekend of our senior undergraduate year to participate in a workshop on prestigious national awards, courtesy of the University of Arkansas's Office of Nationally Competitive Awards. For two days at a conference center in the Missouri Ozarks, we listened to and discussed strategies related to applying and interviewing for the Gates Cambridge, Marshall, Rhodes, and Fulbright Scholarships. Fresh from a wonderful junior year abroad at the University of Cambridge, I was intent on returning for a Master's degree and had resolved to apply for the Gates Cambridge Scholarship.

Already aware of the immense amount of work and effort I would have to put into the paper application, I was surprised at the emphasis given to interviewing skills and techniques during the workshop. "Why are we spending so much time discussing interviews when we haven't even completed our applications or even been shortlisted?" I remember thinking to myself. Having since been successful in the Gates Cambridge Scholarship competition and having subsequently worked at my alma mater as a postgraduate fellowships advisor, I now know the answer to that question. Interviewing for these awards is a tough business, and not for the faint of heart. In many ways it is a survival-of-the-fittest experience, and the earlier the preparation begins, the better. In most cases, waiting until a student is shortlisted (especially in the case of the Marshall and the Rhodes) does not leave sufficient time for ample practice. And even if it does, earlier is almost always better when it comes to preparing for interviews.

In this chapter—a blend of anecdote and instruction—I would like to articulate some of the tips and advice that I have found (and still find) most useful to advisors who are going through the process of preparing a student for a major scholarship interview. My hope is that both advisors and students will find this piece helpful, containing as it does information that I learned as both a student preparing for a Gates Cambridge interview and subsequently as an advisor.

In my view, my interview training was as good as it possibly could have been. That fall we had a number of national scholarship finalists at Arkansas, and our advisor set up practice interviews for us as early as October. After learning in December that my Gates Cambridge application had earned me a spot on the interview shortlist, she stepped it up a notch with numerous practice interviews in January in preparation for my

February interview. In all, I would say I had about ten practice interviews prior to the real thing (although it felt more like hundreds).

As a student the prospect of a postgraduate fellowship interview, while exciting, was unavoidably terrifying. During the retreat the lecture on interviewing effectively replicated the tense mood of its subject; when Dr. Stephen Sheppard, a University of Arkansas law professor with a resounding voice and a reputation for deadly lines of questioning, announced that he would be teaching by example, the atmosphere of passive reception gave way to one of anxiety and panic. And those advisors who have had students endure a national scholarship interview process know that the pressure and nervousness are not the exclusive domain of the student. To be sure, we advisors feel a great deal of pressure in preparing students for interviews that promise to be challenging at best, and downright grueling at worst. Because interviewing skills are, like any other, best acquired through practice and repetition, much of the pressure falls on the advisor to ensure that the student is receiving the best possible training. Only through a series of practice interviews can students learn how to comfortably, or at least gracefully, think under pressure and respond to collegial confrontation.[1] In a way, interviewing can be one of the most refreshing parts of the scholarship application process to the advisor. Although there are limits on how much a student can clarify involvements, experiences, and interests for a given application, theoretically a student can continue to hone interview skills indefinitely.

The most obvious, and certainly the most critical, way in which to prepare for a fellowship interview is to have the student review his or her application for possible questions. Knowing the essays and personal statements inside and out, what sorts of issues they touch on and suggest, and where such issues could lead will cover a lot of ground in terms of preparation.

True to the reputation of Gates Cambridge interviews,[2] the questions I received in my own interview were all quite predictable and clear-cut, with the majority of them coming logically out of my application. The following are those that stood out as the most prominent. Keep in mind that my undergraduate major was music and my research proposal was on film music.

- How is the undergraduate thesis project that you described in your application linked to the research project you have proposed to complete at Cambridge?
- How does studying for a master's degree fit in with your career goals?

- Are your parents musical? How and when did your interests in music develop?
- Why do you think studying film music is so important?
- What led you to co-establish the (University of Arkansas) Society for Adoption Awareness? Why were you interested in this issue?
- What is the most important thing you learned during your summer internship at the Aspen Music Festival?
- What is the biggest problem facing the arts today?

Thanks to the number and range of questions I encountered during my practice interviews, I was relaxed and prepared to respond on a variety of topics. In fact the biggest surprise of the entire interview was that I was not asked the one question that was virtually guaranteed and that I had prepared for more than any other: why do you want to study this subject at Cambridge and nowhere else? My interview panel was already convinced of my proposal for study and did not hold me to defending it, probably because I had already studied at Cambridge for a year. Nonetheless I felt secure because I had carefully thought through my reasons for selecting my program and had experience articulating them.

In reviewing the application for possible questions, it is also important to look for possible holes or weak answers. Just because a student has been selected as a finalist does not mean that the paper application is flawless in the eyes of the committee. Panelists will often use a weak answer as potentially deadly ammunition. The key to the student's defense is knowing in advance where the weaknesses are, and how those weaknesses might be revealed in the interview, and what the strongest responses are to such questions.

In order best to prepare for the confrontation students may encounter, it is critical to be tough with them during their practice sessions. Easy interviews will not be beneficial in the long run, as the interviews for major scholarships will all have at least a question or two that push the student. For several of my practice sessions, my advisor brought in the Honors College dean and one of our toughest law professors, whose approach often left me and the other Gates finalist in shambles. In terms of practice, this was a good thing. If I stumbled on a question, I could count on getting that question again, and I consequently spent a lot of time reflecting between interviews. Answering confrontational and intentionally difficult questions became easier, and by the time the actual interview rolled around, it was (almost) second nature. Although I was not asked the same questions during the actual interview that I had been continually confronted with in Fayetteville—and that was not the intention of the practice interviews—I had become comfortable with interviewing as a form of interaction.

In addition to looking to the application for questions, it is important to cover some more generic interview questions, which can often trip up candidates who have not prepared for them. Questions such as "Can you tell us something about yourself that does not appear in your application? What would you describe as your greatest weakness? If you could have dinner with any person in the world, who would it be and why?" are not unheard of in these interviews. Often panelists will ask a question of this sort as a warm up, but if a student has not prepared to answer such a "softball" question, then the interview can be lackluster from the start.

Recruiting faculty members and staff for the practice interview committees is also critical. In my view the student should interview with a number of different panels so that students do not become too comfortable answering the same people's questions. Having different interviewers will ensure that different questions come up and that similar questions are asked in different ways. The resulting variation of questions will also prompt students to deliver different answers, and consequently they will avoid one of the major pitfalls of repeated practice interviews: sounding rehearsed and robotic. It is also a good idea to recruit a faculty member from the student's area of study to come up with some discipline-specific questions; often one of the panelists in an interview will be well versed enough in a given area to initiate a difficult line of questioning. Sensing such possible questions in advance will allow students to do their homework and be prepared for the questions that, perhaps more than any other, they will be expected to answer.

Concerning the recruitment of panelists for practice interviews, advisors should choose faculty members who both represent the student's scholastic interest as well as some who do not. In many interviews the panelists may have no knowledge of a student's area of expertise, in which case any digression into academic jargon can be detrimental. Having an international relations professor ask a physics major in nonspecialist terms about a specific theory or study proposal will often require the student to express his or her interests in ways that are understandable to nonspecialists—a crucial skill for many of these scholarships and something students might not have done frequently if the majority of their discussions have been with others in their field. Remember, most of these scholarships aim for their students to be ambassadors of sorts of their subjects to the "real world," and if students are overly dialectical in their speech, they will not be as attractive to panelists as those who can discuss their specialties, however technical, in comprehensible terms. (That's not to say if a panelist does happen to share an understanding of the student's discipline and invites a technical discussion that the student should not follow; however, the student should understand that this will not be characteristic of every answer.)

Having a sufficient number of practice sessions is also important in terms of the ability to relax—a critical component for a successful interview.[3] Students should have had enough preparation that they do not seem anxious or excessively nervous. Although it is misleading to say that selection panels look exclusively for type A personalities, interviewers certainly expect candidates to be good verbal communicators for whom building relationships and networking is enjoyable and easy. Gordon Johnson, Provost of the Gates Cambridge Trust, is famous in NAFA circles for saying that candidates should be "robust." Also, many national scholarships are intended for students who aim to be leaders in their discipline—a role requiring excellent communication skills. If a student is so nervous in the interview that he or she cannot sustain a conversation or even give an articulated answer, the panelists will likely wonder about the student's abilities to converse with peers, who will certainly be engaging them in equally confrontational conversations. In interviews, silence is not golden.

In addition to coaching the student through answering questions, advise them on their mental approach to the interview as a whole. A technique that I found useful was to think of the interview as a discussion structured around a series of questions rather than simply an extended line of confrontational interrogation. Going in with this perspective, I found myself more at ease with answering questions, and consequently my tone was more conversational. During my interview the committee members even discussed between themselves about the issues at hand. This sort of dynamic definitely made the interview more relaxed—more like a roundtable discussion.

Finally, make sure that your students understand that most scholarship committees—and the Gates Cambridge especially—are, in addition to a number of other traits, looking for a quality that is sometimes obscured by the focus on achievement and ambition—a realistic self-assessment. In selecting scholars, the Gates Cambridge Trust notes that the ideal candidates will exhibit, among other traits, "an appropriate humility that comes from an awareness that nothing is ever really simple."[4] Although panelists have a number of ways to probe for this trait, a critical piece of advice to give students is that it is absolutely appropriate, and even preferable, for them to admit that they do not know the answer to a question if that is in fact the case. This is perhaps the simplest way that an interviewer will probe for this trait. Tara Yglesias, Deputy Secretary of the Truman Scholarship, has noted that she often will follow a line of questioning that she knows will eventually lead candidates to say that they do not know enough about the topic to answer the question. Although saying "I just don't know" to a committee might feel like a moment of failure to students, such a demonstration of modesty in most cases will actually be attractive to the panelists. Despite the vibes they might give, interviewers do not expect students to know the answer to every question. They do, however, expect them to recognize and admit the limits of their knowledge, and in most interviews, will make sure they are able to do so.

The advisor is responsible for learning as much as possible about the scholarship a given candidate is interviewing for and the tendencies of that scholarship's interviews. No two fellowship interviews are the same, and interviews for different scholarships certainly have different expectations; some scholarships (the Gates Cambridge, for instance) are known for keeping interview questions in the domain of the student's discipline and having a relatively friendly atmosphere; others tend to be more confrontational, with questioning that can wander into areas in which the student is not well informed. These reputations are no secrets, and seasoned NAFA members, veteran advisors, and many foundations will be happy to share expert advice on how best to prepare students for a given interview.

Students understand that the interview process is subjective. Unfortunately, many perfectly qualified and even ideal candidates are often overlooked. I was very lucky in that I had completed a year of study at Cambridge as a junior and had a very supportive letter of recommendation from one of the faculty members there—a circumstance that likely led my particular committee to feel that Cambridge was unquestionably the right place for me. These interviews (and the entire application process for that matter) are often driven by tremendous amounts of luck and circumstance, with external factors having a hand in a committee's decision to grant scholarships to specific candidates and withhold them from others. Speaking of such "external factors," I would like to close by recounting how one seemingly unrelated circumstance came into play during my interview, fortunately to my advantage.

The first question I was asked when I sat down at the interview table was a rather strange one: so, did you get any takers on your crab cake dinner? I'll explain. After I had arrived at the hotel in Annapolis the evening before, I, like all the candidates, had registered in the hotel's conference room in order to get my welcome letter, interview time, hotel key, and so forth. I was also informed that I could, if I wished, write a message on the large white message board sitting on an easel in the room. The purpose of this board was for us to open the lines of communication so that we could get groups together to go out to eat and socialize for the night. I did not really want to sit in my room or eat dinner alone, so I left a message—the first in fact—for other finalists: "Crab Cakes Anyone?" (Remember our proximity to the Chesapeake.)

As it turned out, many others wanted crab cakes as well, and the evening turned into a jovial social outing. (The crab cakes were great as well.) So why, you might ask, did the committee ask about this, much less know about it? Well, as luck would have it, the committee members met for breakfast the morning of the interviews in the very room in which we had registered, complete with the white message board that had been left overnight. Having seen my message, my committee used it as an ice-breaking intro. Though I wouldn't say that this circumstance singlehandedly won me the scholarship, it certainly led to a conversational atmosphere at the outset of the interview, calming my nerves.

I suppose the moral of this story is that even though these interviews seemed to be closed (i.e., ones that were not supplemented by other activities such as the reception at the Rhodes interviews), there are still ways and means by which the interview extended outside the bounds of the "official" twenty minutes. Though circumstantial, my situation made it clear that I was eager to meet the other candidates and socialize in a group setting. This bit of serendipity paid off in the end, demonstrating that any "unofficial" contact—direct or indirect—with panelists before interviews will likely be remembered and, for better or worse, may even be taken into account when the time for final decisions arrives.

At the end of the day, advisors should simply urge students to go into the interview aiming to have a great experience. Through the process they will surely have learned a great deal about themselves and will also have garnered some great interview skills, which will be useful for whatever they end up doing in the future. Whatever the outcome, make sure they remember that they are fortunate to have made it to the interview stage; hundreds apply, and few proceed. They, *and* you, should be proud.

10

Involving Faculty in the Scholarship Effort

KARNA WALTER

Karna Walter is Director of Nationally Competitive Scholarships in the Honors College at the University of Arizona. She earned a BA in English from Calvin College in 1993 and subsequently served there as an admissions counselor. She completed a PhD in higher education at the University of Arizona in 2000 and then served as Assistant Director of International Studies and Scholarships in the University of Arizona Honors College before assuming her current position in 2004. She serves on the Faculty Advisory Board for International Studies and coordinates several series sponsored by the Honors College. She also teaches an honors course on human trafficking and is part of an Arizona-wide network of people addressing the problem of human trafficking.

The campus deadline is nearing, and you are working feverishly with outstanding students who aspire to study or do research overseas supported by one of the British awards, or by way of a Fulbright Scholarship. As the deadlines approach, you realize that you do not yet have enough faculty members who have agreed to assist with your interview processes.

You also realize that you have worked almost singlehandedly with your applicants—and you have continued the ongoing process of looking for additional qualified students to apply—for the past year. You would love to have more help and be able to direct students confidently for advice on their candidacies and applications. You recognize that you always ask the same small subset of faculty members to assist with just about everything, and it occurs to you that there must be a better way. But what is it?

At the 2007 NAFA Conference in Washington, DC, a panel of scholarship professionals addressed this question, talking about different models of faculty involvement on their campuses. The panelists represented different types of institutions: a small, private institution in the DC area; a mid-sized public institution in Virginia; a formerly-private-now-public institution in Pennsylvania, and a large, state institution in Arizona. Though the institutions were very different, involving energetic, informed faculty in the scholarship process was a high priority for each one.

We had no "one-size-fits-all" approach to offer, but each of us responded to similar questions about what we have tried to do to create strong faculty partnerships. Each of our settings is unique, requiring a customized way of identifying key faculty members to assist in recruitment and advising efforts. But whether advisors work at a small liberal arts college, a big public university, or somewhere in between, they likely face the same question every year—how do advisors engage faculty actively in scholarship work and reward them when they participate? Before addressing this question, examining why faculty members are so necessary to the success of our mission can help put the question in context.

Faculty as Key Partners

It may seem self-evident that faculty members are critical to our work as scholarship professionals. Indeed some scholarship professionals are also faculty members who understand the dimensions of academic disciplines and departments as well as anyone. Faculty member or not, additional faculty partners are a key component of a successful office and are important partners in advancing scholarship efforts across the campus. Several reasons come into play:

- Faculty members are most closely connected to students because they interact with them in classrooms and in performance and research spaces. This relationship allows them to identify talented students early, especially those in their area of inquiry, and assist the students in effectively examining their long-term interests and goals. They can also often identify leaders in and outside the classroom.
- Professors who become invested in the process can work cooperatively with the scholarship office, directing students to the appropriate personnel to learn more about specific opportunities.
- Faculty can lend their expertise during application reviews and interviews.
- Faculty members have access to other faculty, administrators, and professionals who may not otherwise connect with scholarship directors, which can assist the office in building faculty networks and multiplying the number of committed faculty who can help identify both exceptional students and additional scholarship partners.
- More indirectly, top faculty can create an intellectual ethos that will help attract prospective students who may be future scholarship contenders.

The right faculty members can be critical colleagues in scholarship efforts. They can identify and connect us with outstanding scholarship candidates, offer their intellectual skill during our application processes, and connect us to their potentially vast networks of faculty members and administrators who can help us to extend our partnerships across campus. Whether our institutions are big or small, we can all benefit from strengthening our networks to include as many prospective applicants as well as faculty and staff partners as possible.

Partnering Models

Clearly, creating robust partnerships with faculty members is an important part of our work as scholarship professionals. Now comes the practical part: how do we engage them? Before we can establish productive relationships with faculty members, we need to think about the context in which we do our work.

KEY QUESTIONS

Our panel addressed several key questions that we will consider in turn. The first question concerns how the reporting structure affects access to faculty. Some directors report to the campus president or provost, or perhaps to the dean of a liberal arts and sciences college. Others may be housed in an honors college or office and report to the honors dean or director. Others are located in a career center, and there are many other arrangements. Thinking about the existing reporting structure is helpful in strategizing the best way to connect with faculty. Would it work to seek assistance from the president, provost, or dean in asking faculty to serve on scholarship committees or to assist in some other way? Given the current campus climate, would this be untenable? Being savvy about the implications of reporting structures will help in thinking through the best way to engage faculty on campus.

Our panel considered another important question: what institutional idiosyncrasies make a home institution unique and potentially problematic? Understanding how and why the school began, its stated mission, the socioeconomic profile, the number of students (undergraduate and graduate), and department/discipline strengths will be very useful in knowing how to move forward in engaging faculty. Those of us who have worked on our campuses for a long time are likely to be aware of campus complexities and how they play out. Professionals new to a campus may have a more difficult time distilling these unique qualities at first. Yet gaining an understanding—and learning how to navigate campus politics and idiosyncrasies—is an important part of developing a strong foothold at any institution.

For a director or coordinator new to a campus, making connections is critical. Talking with staff in peer positions is a good way to begin. Working lunches can help. Consider inviting out, individually first and later in groups, directors of related divisions:

- Study Abroad Office
- Undergraduate Research Office
- Libraries (especially those with internship programs)
- Honors College or Honors Office
- Multicultural Center

- Career Services
- Academic Scholarship Office (or the equivalent office providing merit awards for incoming freshmen and current students)
- Financial Aid Office
- Admissions
- First-Year Experience
- Pre-College Programs

The directors of these offices will be important partners in helping identify students early who demonstrate academic and leadership potential. They will also help make connections to faculty and will likely understand and be willing to share information about campus strengths and individual faculty engagement.

After assessing what is currently available at the institution, advisors need to assess their own backgrounds. How might it shape the work at hand? Socioeconomic characteristics come into play: gender, ethnicity, age, and the like. Professional characteristics also arise because some of us are faculty who may have networks with faculty members from home departments or units. Others of us do not have faculty status but may still have built-in connections with faculty members. Still others may not have easy-to-tap ties with faculty members and must rely instead on key relationships with supervisors, individual faculty, or peer directors who can pave the way to engage faculty.

The higher education background that an individual advisor brings to the office will necessarily shape the direction the office takes. Some professionals have experience on one kind of campus: large state institutions, say, or small liberal arts colleges. Some may have a variety of professional experiences on a variety of campuses. Others may have attended one type of institution but now work at another. That is my story: I attended a small private college in the Midwest and now work in a large public university in the Southwest. Although there are certain commonalities among institutions of higher education, the two institutions where I have spent the most time are very different on many levels. If I expected my current institution to mirror the other—which is religiously affiliated, small, and focused almost exclusively on under-graduates—I would be ill-prepared to serve students at my current institution. Adapting to the specific environment, then, is very important.

Identifying Faculty

As we understand our institutional context and how we can operate effectively within it, we gain a better understanding of who our key faculty partners could be and how best to approach them. Our best colleagues may be longtime faculty with a broad institutional memory and numerous connections across campus. Or they might be new, young faculty with a fresh energy and enthusiasm. Perhaps our best colleagues are faculty with interdisciplinary interests that allow them to forge relationships of breadth and depth on campus. Or we may call upon former scholarship applicants/winners who are now faculty members on our campus.

Once we determine how to approach those who could best serve, we should develop specific ideas for what we want them to do. Faculty can help in the usual ways: by serving on review committees and interview panels and by providing suggestions about prospective applicants. But there may be fresh ways of engaging faculty in our work that may be mutually beneficial.

My campus is a public institution with an enrollment of 37,000 students (28,000 undergraduates). After a few years of scholarship work, I realized how challenging it was to reach the entire campus with the scholarship message. I am housed in the Honors College at my university, so I have access to many of the best students on our campus. Because my office works with any student, regardless of whether a student is affiliated with the Honors College, I found it nearly impossible to identify prospective applicants outside of the Honors College. I also did not have a long history on campus or extensive connections with faculty. I knew I needed to do something.

To address these challenges, I created the Scholarship Advisory Board, which comprises several faculty members from different disciplines across campus. In speaking with key individuals—the dean of the Honors College, as well as academic deans, associate deans, and faculty within different departments—I identified a short list of faculty members to serve on this board. After considering and meeting with many good faculty prospects, I created a four-person board that would be broadly representative of academic disciplines, years of experience, and socioeconomic characteristics.

The board is charged with making presentations to appropriate student and faculty groups about scholarship opportunities, briefing these same people about upcoming workshops and deadlines, meeting individually with prospective applicants, and coleading our annual board breakfast (we invite faculty, administrators, and advisors in order to educate them about our scholarship efforts). The four faculty members are appointed to three-year terms, with one or two people rotating off each year, and each board member receives a stipend for his or her work.

Launching the board was helpful in both widening and deepening our scholarship efforts on campus, creating synergies among different units that have been mutually beneficial. The board also provides training to faculty new to the scholarship process on approaching students appropriately, on the ethics of advising and mentoring them through the application process, and on assisting applicants who do not ultimately receive awards.

The number of campus presentations, scholarship applicants, and, yes, scholarship recipients has increased in the past few years. And because its membership changes every year with at least one member rotating off, the board is infused with new energy and enthusiasm for our collective tasks. This model may not fit well on every campus, but it may stimulate ideas that fit other institutional contexts.

Faculty members are an indispensable part of our work in the academy, and it behooves scholarship professionals to forge strong relationships with key faculty as we undertake scholarship work. To maintain productive relationships, it is important to recognize faculty efforts. News releases announcing finalists and award recipients should include the students' faculty mentors. Small stipends go a long way in sustaining faculty members who consistently provide dedicated support. Letters of thanks to interview panelists and recommenders from the provost, chancellor, or president make clear to faculty members their efforts are appreciated at the highest levels. Receptions, dinners, and awards recognizing exceptional commitments on the part of faculty are also an important part of a vibrant relationship.

Understanding our unique institutional context is an important first step in effectively seeking out and deploying faculty members who can help us multiply our efforts. Clearly we have something to gain from their expertise, experience, and mentoring ability. But let us not forget that scholarship professionals have something valuable to offer faculty, too. We can become the "go-to" people who can provide information and historic understanding of what it takes to assist our very best students in pursuing worthy goals. Nurturing these students is an important way for us to work hand in hand with faculty. We both have students' best interests at heart. In the best possible world, we will create and sustain strong, mutually beneficial ties with faculty members that will benefit them, us, and the students we hope to attract to our campuses.[1]

11

Undergraduate Research Revisited
Resources for Faculty and Opportunities for Students

LAURA DAMUTH

Laura Damuth is Director of Undergraduate Research and Fellowship
Advising at the University of Nebraska-Lincoln. She holds a BA from Vassar
College, MA, MPhil, and PhD degrees in historical musicology from
Columbia University, and teaches classes on music history in the university's
honors program. Dr. Damuth was hired by the University of
Nebraska-Lincoln in 1999 to administer the Undergraduate Creative
Activity and Research Program (UCARE). Under her guidance, UCARE has
grown to nearly 400 undergraduate students working with over
350 University of Nebraska-Lincoln faculty members. Her own research
interests revolve around the Italian cantata in the seventeenth and
eighteenth centuries, most specifically those of Alessandro Scarlatti. In 2004
she became the university's fellowships advisor, overseeing all of the major
scholarships and fellowships; this last fall she was also named Fulbright
Program Advisor.

In the past few years, the undergraduate research landscape has been changing. More institutions are involving students in research as undergraduates, and the number of opportunities for students and resources for faculty has been steadily on the rise. At times information on these developments can seem overwhelming and somewhat confusing. Google undergraduate research and 2,920,000 different sites will quickly be available for review. Putting this information in some sort of perspective is essential. Key factors addressed here include resources for administrators, faculty, and staff; research opportunities for undergraduates through federal funding; and opportunities for students to present their work. What follows is by no means a comprehensive list of resources, but it may serve as a place to start for fellowships advisors who want to assist in connecting their students to research opportunities.

Resources for Administrators/Faculty/Staff

Two main national organizations—the Council on Undergraduate Research and the Reinvention Center—strongly advocate for undergraduate research. Their Web sites are helpful, providing detailed information and links to other extremely useful resources. The National Collegiate Honors Council also promotes undergraduate research, offering an opportunity for students to make presentations at its conference and providing a variety of publications that any advisor looking to expand undergraduate research opportunities for students will find helpful.

THE COUNCIL ON UNDERGRADUATE RESEARCH (CUR)

Established in 1978, the Council on Undergraduate Research (CUR) has been a strong advocate and supporter of undergraduate research, promoting "high quality undergraduate student-faculty collaborative research and scholarship." Originally a grassroots organization created by science faculty at predominantly undergraduate institutions, CUR has grown to embrace multiple disciplines (science, math, engineering, social sciences, and soon the arts and humanities) and all institutions that have a focus on undergraduate education, including research-focused universities. As the council's Web site states:

CUR provides support for faculty development. Our publications and outreach activities are designed to share successful models and strategies for establishing and institutionalizing undergraduate research programs. We assist administrators and faculty members in improving and assessing the research environment at their institutions. CUR also provides information on the importance of undergraduate research to state legislatures, private foundations, government agencies, and the US Congress.

I have found the CUR publications to be invaluable. The *CUR Quarterly*, which comes out in September, December, March, and June, is the "public voice" of CUR and provides useful information to its members and the wider academic community. Over the past few years, the *CUR Quarterly* has had such themes as NSF research at undergraduate institutions, undergraduate research in the humanities and social sciences, and creating time for research, as well as articles on the Howard Hughes Medical Institute Awards. The most recent *CUR Quarterly* has the theme models of undergraduate research, with many insightful articles on community-based research and interdisciplinary research.

CUR also hosts a biannual national conference and special institutes that address many topics concerning undergraduate research. For example, upcoming CUR institute topics are: "Initiating and Sustaining Undergraduate Research Programs," "Beginning a Research Program in the Natural Sciences at a Predominantly Undergraduate Institution," "Institutionalizing Undergraduate Research," "Proposal Writing," and "Mentorship, Collaboration and Undergraduate Research in the Social Sciences and Humanities." These are usually two- to three-day meetings on a college campus. Often institutions send teams of individuals to meet and discuss these issues. Another opportunity, *CUR Dialogues,* is designed to bring faculty and administrators to the Washington, DC, area to interact with federal agency program officers and other grant funders. There are also a number of professional services offered by CUR: a consulting service, a mentor network, the CUR Listserv, and more.

One CUR publication that I found extremely useful as I was developing our undergraduate research program at the University of Nebraska-Lincoln was Toufic M. Hakim's *At the Interface of Scholarship and Teaching: How to Develop and Administer Institutional Undergraduate Research Programs* (CUR, July 2000). This small monograph provides practical advice, developed from years of experience, on how to develop and sustain a campus undergraduate research initiative.[1]

THE REINVENTION CENTER

The Reinvention Center, located at the University of Miami,[2] is a national center concentrating on all aspects of undergraduate education at research universities. The name of the center is generated from the Boyer Commission Report, *Reinventing Undergraduate Education: A Blueprint for America's Research Universities* (1998).[3] The most recent focus of the Reinvention Center has been the importance of undergraduate research and the way research can be integrated into the undergraduate experience at a large research institution. The center promotes "best practices" and sponsors a biannual meeting as well as smaller regional workshops. Its Web site explains:

> *While many good ideas have taken hold on individual campuses and within individual disciplines, research universities do not have any organizations that focus on their specific needs and challenges or provide a forum that enables them to profit from one another's experiences. The Reinvention Center has formed regional networks made up of research university faculty and administrators to fill this gap. The networks meet on a regular basis to discuss key issues, share experiences and work toward achieving common goals.*

The Web site is particularly useful, with sections on upcoming events, regional networks, studies, and a "spotlight" section. Some of the topics recently covered in the Reinvention Center's spotlight are: "Creative Uses of Instructional Technology," "Engaging Humanities Students in Research," Application of Quantitative Concepts and Techniques in Undergraduate Biology," "The Minor as a Vehicle for Interdisciplinary Education," "Undergraduate Research, Scholarship, and Creative Activity," "First-Year Initiatives," and "Achieving an Interdisciplinary General Education." Sprinkled throughout the Web site are important resources on particular topics related to undergraduate education, and often specifically on undergraduate research. For example there are bibliographies on such topics as assessment, collaborative learning, community-based teaching and learning, and computer-based teaching, and these are only a few resources available.[4]

NATIONAL COLLEGIATE HONORS COUNCIL (NCHC)

Although this organization is focused on honors education—and undergraduate research is only a part of that—NCHC does provide support and resources for faculty who are involved with honors programs and the senior thesis. NCHC's annual national conference provides a number of different opportunities for faculty to learn about different kinds of research models. Honors students as well as faculty and staff are invited to this conference and can present the results of their research. NCHC also generates a number of different publications: *The Journal of the National Collegiate Honors Council* (a periodical with articles on honors education), *Honors in Practice* (a publication that focuses on the "nuts and bolts" of honors topics), and NCHC Monographs, with publications such as *Assessing and Evaluating Honors Programs and Honors Colleges: A Practical Handbook to Innovations in Undergraduate Research and Honors Education*. All of these include advice, best practices, descriptions of successful honors classes and out-of-classroom experiences, and models for honors education.

NCHC also offers faculty institutes and development opportunities. This particular organization is not for all institutions, but whether or not a campus has an honors college or program, NCHC can provide a wealth of information and support for high-achieving students.[5]

Research Opportunities for Undergraduates through Federal Funding

Federally funded undergraduate research grants offer students the opportunity to expand their research experiences at sites other than their own campus. These grants generally provide at least funding for housing with a living stipend, and they sometimes also provide funds for travel. Such research experiences are very important to student development. Students competing for Goldwater, Truman, Udall, and a host of graduate scholarship opportunities have often participated in one of these programs.

NATIONAL AERONAUTICS AND SPACE ADMINISTRATION (NASA) UNDERGRADUATE STUDENT RESEARCH PROGRAM (USRP)

The National Aeronautics and Space Administration offers internships year-round at all NASA facilities. Selected students receive a stipend and round-trip travel allowance. Students may apply for a fifteen-week spring session, a ten-week summer session, or a fifteen-week fall session. Undergraduates with an academic major or course concentration in engineering, mathematics, computer science, or physical and life sciences who are U.S. citizens enrolled full-time in accredited U.S. colleges or universities are eligible to apply. NASA-USRP provides students with hands-on experiences with NASA scientists and engineers.[6]

NATIONAL SCIENCE FOUNDATION (NSF) RESEARCH EXPERIENCES FOR UNDERGRADUATES (REU)

The NSF provides a number of Research Experiences for Undergraduates (REU) and is one of the largest federal agencies that funds undergraduate research. There are essentially two kinds of support:

1. *REU sites* are located at a variety of different university settings and in a variety of different disciplines supported by the NSF. Students become involved with ongoing research and apply directly to the REU site. These sites may be in a single discipline or in multiple departments with a complementary intellectual theme. Proposals with an international dimension are also possible.[7]
2. *REU Supplements* may be requested for ongoing NSF-funded research projects or may be included as a component of proposals for new or renewal NSF grants or cooperative agreements.[8]

NATIONAL INSTITUTES OF HEALTH (NIH) UNDERGRADUATE SCHOLARSHIP PROGRAM

The NIH, headquartered in a suburb of Washington, DC, is a component of the U.S. Department of Health and Human Services and is the world's largest biomedical research institution. It has at least two undergraduate programs to which students can apply:

1. *NIH Undergraduate Scholarship Program* offers awards to students from disadvantaged backgrounds, committed to health-related research careers in biomedical, behavioral, and social science. The program offers scholarship support—up to $20,000 per academic year in tuition educational expenses and reasonable living expenses to scholarship recipients—paid ten-week research training

at the NIH during the summer, and paid employment at the NIH after graduation.

2. *NIH Summer Internship Program in Biomedical Research* provides an opportunity for undergraduates to spend the summer working on biomedical research. Students sixteen years of age or older who are U.S. citizens or permanent residents and are currently enrolled at least half-time in high school, an accredited U.S. college or university, or an accredited U.S. medical/dental school are eligible to apply. Students who have been accepted into a college or university may also apply. [9]

NATIONAL INSTITUTE OF STANDARDS AND TECHNOLOGY (NIST) SUMMER UNDERGRADUATE RESEARCH FELLOWSHIP (SURF) PROGRAMS

The National Institute of Standards and Technology's Gaithersburg, MD, Summer Undergraduate Research Fellowship (SURF) program is designed for students majoring in science, mathematics, or engineering. The applications for participation in the SURF program are only accepted from colleges or universities, and not from individual students. Candidates prepare a single proposal from the institution to the NIST SURF program. There are nine NIST laboratories: Building and Fire Research, Center for Nanoscale Science and Technology, Chemical Science and Technology, Electronics and Electrical Engineering, Information Technology, Manufacturing Engineering, Materials Science and Engineering, NIST Center for Neutron Research, and Physics.

The student application form will indicate which laboratory the student is most interested in. The applications will be considered by all programs, with consideration of the student's preferences and research interests. There is also a NIST site in Boulder, CO, which operates a SURF program with a separate application required.[10]

DEPARTMENT OF ENERGY SCIENCE UNDERGRADUATE RESEARCH LABORATORY INTERNSHIPS

This program places students in paid internships in science and engineering at any of several Department of Energy facilities. Students work with scientists or engineers on projects related to the laboratories' research programs, and each lab offers different research opportunities.

The summer programs at the various laboratories run from late May to mid-August, fall programs run from August through December, and spring programs from January through May. The exact start date will depend on the laboratory and will be given to participants who have been accepted at that specific laboratory. Students are required to participate for the full term of the program.[11]

Opportunities for Students to Present Their Work

Presenting posters or papers at a regional or national conference is invaluable experience for undergraduates. Conferences provide students with the opportunity to network with peers and faculty in their fields. Students develop presentation skills, and the experience builds confidence and poise.

NATIONAL CONFERENCES ON UNDERGRADUATE RESEARCH (NCUR)

This annual conference, open to all undergraduates in all disciplines, draws over 2,000 students and their faculty mentors to present their research through posters, oral presentations, visual arts, and performances. A conference proceedings of selected student papers is also published. As the NCUR Web site states:

> *Student presentations are welcome in all fields and disciplines from the creative and performing arts to biomedical, engineering, and social science research. The National Conferences on Undergraduate Research provides a wonderful opportunity for your students: (1) to meet peers and faculty from around the country working in similar research fields; (2) to learn about how research and scholarship is conducted in a wide range of fields from the humanities and creative arts to the life sciences and engineering; (3) to learn about graduate school and employment opportunities from our presenters; and (4) to develop presentation skills. All student abstracts and applications will be reviewed by a faculty committee from the host institution. Students presenting at the National Conference have the option of doing either an oral or poster presentation.*

The national conference also offers some sessions for faculty and administrators. These FAN (Faculty and Administrators Network) sessions often focus on "best practices" and also provide an opportunity for faculty and administrators from all over the country to meet and share information.[12]

CUR UNDERGRADUATE RESEARCH POSTERS ON THE HILL

CUR also hosts an annual undergraduate research poster session on Capitol Hill, "Posters on the Hill," usually in late March or early April. Sixty competitively selected posters are displayed in the U.S. Capitol during a late-afternoon reception.[13]

This is not intended to be a complete listing of resources for faculty, administrators, or students. It is simply a place to begin to start learning more about the developments over the past few years concerning undergraduate research. I strongly encourage advisors interested in research opportunities to visit the Web sites listed in the notes section and to consider joining the relevant organizations included. I have found that these organizations (especially CUR and the Reinvention Center) have been instrumental in furthering my understanding of undergraduate research and have helped me to be a better undergraduate research program director. My CUR colleagues gave critical advice and support when I was shaping the UCARE (Undergraduate Creative Activities and Research Experiences) Program here at the University of Nebraska-Lincoln.

Notes

Introduction

1. Derek Bok, *Our Underachieving Colleges: A Candid Look at How Much Students Learn and Why They Should Be Learning More* (Princeton: Princeton University Press, 2008), p. 236.

2. Bok, *Our Underachieving Colleges*, p. 237.

Chapter One: State Department Initiatives for International Academic Exchange

1. This essay is based on Ms. Craven's keynote address at the National Association of Fellowships Advisors in Washington, DC, in July 2007.

2. I want to express our sincere appreciation for the work fellowships advisors, those in NAFA in particular, do to inform, encourage, and guide American students in seeking scholarships to participate in international study, as well as their commitment to the importance of academic and cultural exchange between the United States and other countries.

3. This refers to participants in 2007.

4. The MTVU 2008 award recipients include:

> **Melissa Adams,** who graduated from Emory University with a Masters in Public Health, will travel to Uganda to work on a hip-hop therapy project in which youth affected by war and by AIDS in Northern Uganda learn to beatbox, break dance, compose positive rap songs, and create hip-hop beats with local instruments. She will conduct an assessment of the children's needs and available resources and will use the data to determine how best to further meet their psychosocial needs through these therapeutic resources.
>
> **Ainsley Breault,** who will graduate from the University of Southern California with a BA in Communication and a minor in Cinema-Television, will travel to New Zealand to research the role of music in perpetuating Maori culture. She will conclude the project by obtaining a one-year certificate in Maori music at Auckland University of

Technology and will chronicle two significant Maori music events, sharing her findings through two 30-minute rockumentary-style digital videos.

Katherine Good, who graduated Phi Beta Kappa from Loyola University Chicago with a BS in Anthropology and a BA in International Studies, will travel to Mexico to produce podcasts that anthropologically explore the Mexican youth renaissance of performing various pre-rock music styles. A folk musician and independent radio producer, Katherine will work with the School of Mexican Music in Mexico City and the *danzon* and *son jarocho* circles of Veracruz to document this growing cultural trend.

Spencer Orey, who will graduate from the University of California, Berkeley, with a BA in Anthropology, will travel to Mali to study the rich tradition of *griot* musicians, who are considered living embodiments of cultural knowledge. He will research the roles musicians played in the Malian transition to democracy and what roles they play currently. From his findings, he will create a compilation CD of music. See http://2001–2009.state.gov/r/pa/prs/ps/2008/jun/105822.htm for information.

Alexis Tucker, who will graduate from Princeton University with a BA in French and African Studies, will travel to France to study how socially engaged French rap music and hip-hop culture have addressed the aftermath of the 2005 riots and the 2007 French presidential election. She will produce a multimedia presentation and a documentary that reflect the political role of hip-hop in France.

Chapter Two: *Non Ducor, Duco:* Leadership and the Truman Scholarship Application

1. "I am not led, I lead." This is the city motto of Sao Paulo, Brazil. An expansive definition of leadership would necessarily require that we look to the people who perfected the bikini for guidance.

2. This material is adapted from a 2007 NAFA conference presentation. Thanks to Jane Curlin, Mary Denyer, and Scott Henderson for participating in that presentation and providing many of the best ideas outlined in this paper.

3. This number typically represents a much smaller number of schools since many faculty representatives request information on more than one candidate.

4. The foundation receives approximately 600 applications per year. This number is fairly constant, in part because colleges and universities are limited to only four applications per school (excluding transfer students). We review over 200 files annually.

5. The text of the question is as follows: "Describe one specific example of your leadership. Limit to 2,000 characters including spaces."

6. These questions ask for a listing of high school and college activities, public and community service activities, and political or governmental activities.

7. Question 8 asks the student to describe a compelling example of his or her public service.

Chapter Three: How Soon Is Too Soon? Identifying Qualified Candidates

1. A list of NSPA members is posted at www.scholarshipproviders.org.

2. Various authors, *I Have Risen: Essays by African American Youth* (Berkeley: University of California Press, 2002).

3. http://www.ronbrown.org/cgi-bin/profile.cgi?user_id=36

4. See http://www.mitchellinstitute.org/.

Chapter Four: The National Institutes of Health/Oxford/Cambridge Scholars Program: A New Approach to Biomedical PhD Training

1. National Institutes of Health/Oxford/Cambridge Scholars Program Scholarships in the National Institutes of Health/Oxford/Cambridge Scholars Program are offered to exceptionally promising students who wish to pursue accelerated PhD or MD/PhD training at the cutting edge of biomedical research in collaborative projects between labs of the National Institutes of Health and Oxford University or Cambridge University. These scholarships fully fund PhD training expenses, including tuition, college fees, stipend, health insurance, and travel. Scholars can receive full funding for combined MD/PhD training in coordination with one of the 42 top U.S. medical schools that have NIH-funded Medical Scientist Training Programs.

NIH/Oxford/Cambridge Scholars carry out research in both the United States and the United Kingdom in any area of biomedical inquiry of their choosing. Training includes opportunities for multidisciplinary research and experiences that place medical research in the context of the broader social fabric. NIH/Oxford/Cambridge Scholars, on average, complete their PhD training in four years. Applicants must be U.S. citizens and have completed a bachelor's degree. Students with strong backgrounds in the traditional areas of biomedical studies, as well as in computer science, engineering, mathematics, and physics, are encouraged to apply.
Web site: http://oxcam.gpp.nih.gov

Chapter Six: Creating Opportunities for Experiential Education in a Resource-Strained Environment

1. Several of my colleagues provided invaluable assistance in preparing this essay: Dr. Francine Blume, Director of Experiential Education, American University Career Center; Ms. Marcy Fink Campos, Director, American University Community Service Center; Prof. Leena Jayaswal, Head of the Photography

Concentration, American University School of Communication; and Dr. Adeyemi Stembridge, Director, American University Collaborative for Urban Education Research and Development, School of Education, Teaching, and Health.

2. American University's academic regulations for internships are available at http://www.american.edu/careercenter/faculty/internships/regulations.html.

3. Information about the "Invitation to Dream" youth summit series and a copy of the report the students generated are available at http://www.dcvoice.org.

4. This list is not exhaustive; it is intended to illustrate the various kinds of resources that may be useful to scholarships advisors who wish to explore ways of encouraging experiential education on their campuses.

Chapter Seven: A Newcomer's Guide to Scholarship Advising

1. Jim Hohenbary compiled a set of sample materials, including tips on writing the personal statement and letters to candidates who have not advanced in the competition, for the Boot Camp workshop. Those materials are available on the National Association of Fellowships Advisors Web page: http://www.nafadvisors.org/.

2. The information in this chapter is based on presentations and discussions at the Boot Camp preconference workshop at the NAFA Conference in Washington, DC, in July 2007. My fellow presenters included Laura Damuth, University of Nebraska-Lincoln; Jim Duban, University of North Texas; Paula Goldsmid, Pomona College; Lisa Grimes, College of William and Mary; and Jim Hohenbary, Kansas State University. Also involved in the session, which included nine facilitated breakouts, were Deirdre Moloney, George Mason University; Beth Powers, University of Illinois at Chicago; Dana Vredeveld, Ohio State University; and Judy Zang, Carnegie Mellon University.

3. I will take the author's prerogative to encourage fellowships advisors, new or experienced, to read William Cronon's "Only Connect" [William Cronon, "'Only Connect . . .' The Goals of a Liberal Arts Education," *The American Scholar,* 67 (Autumn 1988): 73–80]. I find the article to be the savviest piece I have read in many years about a liberal arts education and have used it as a basis of discussion with both faculty and students. The attributes of an educated person that Cronon discusses and how he approaches that discussion resonate with me as I think about the qualities many foundations articulate they are seeking in candidates for their awards. These qualities include being able to listen to others and truly hear, reading and understanding widely, crafting thought into effective speaking and writing, solving a wide variety of qualitative and quantitative problems, respecting rigor as a "way of seeking truth," practicing "humility, tolerance, and self-criticism," knowing how to accomplish goals, and working to make those around us better and stronger. Taken from E. M. Forster's novel *Howard's End,* Cronon's culminating point is "*Only Connect . . .*" That is, ultimately, a liberal arts education is about "gaining the power and the wisdom, the generosity and the freedom to connect" and to make

communities better in a multitude of ways. Being effective in what we do on our campuses means connecting in the ways Cronon articulates—connecting to the ideals of the institution and to the wide range of constituents who can make good things happen.

Chapter Eight: Encouraged to Apply: Diversity and the Scholarship Process

1. http://www.rochester.edu/president/memos/2007/faculty_senate.html

2. http://www.union.edu/Admissions/union_at_a_glance/index.php

3. http://www.uic.edu/depts/oae/docs/Campus%20Diversity%20Profile%202008.pdf

4. It is probably not lost on the reader that the director of the Office of Special Scholarship Programs, working with undergraduate and professional students, is Beth Powers. Not only does the University of Illinois at Chicago have two offices to work with students in applying for these fellowships, one of those advisors is a founding board member and former president of NAFA, with over ten years of experience in recruiting and very successfully advising underrepresented students.

5. From the page http://www.nsfgrfp.org/about_the_program/statistics_and_past_recipients:

The National Science Foundation strives to enlist committed individuals who have the characteristics and skills necessary to advance the fields of science and engineering. Maximizing the diversity of leaders in the science and engineering community is important, as diversity is essential in ensuring future access to and participation from historically under-represented groups. NSF welcomes and encourages applications from all U.S. citizens, nationals and permanent residents, including those who belong to underrepresented populations in the sciences, those with disabilities, and people from all geographic and economic backgrounds.

Ethnic Diversity of 2008 Reviewed Applications*

African American	3.4%
Asian	10.2%
Native Hawaiian or Other Pacific Islander	0.2%
Native American	0.6%
Caucasian	72.3%
Multi-Ethnic	1.9%
Hispanic or Latino	5.9%
No Response	9.4%

*Includes all submitted applications including those deemed ineligible after submission.

6. http://www.ed.gov/programs/jacobjavits/performance.html

7. http://us.fulbrightonline.org/thinking_competition.html

8. Michael T. Nettles and Catherine M. Millett, *Three Magic Letters: Getting to PhD* (Baltimore: The Johns Hopkins University Press, 2006).

Chapter Nine: Preparing for *the* Interview: Advice from a Gates Cambridge Scholar and Fellowships Advisor

1. On occasion, an advisor might have a student who is naturally gifted at interviewing and for whom too much practice will actually inhibit ability. While rare, I have observed this myself, specifically with a candidate who interviewed for and won a major national scholarship.

2. Interviews for the Gates Cambridge Scholarships are among the most transparent of the major scholarship interviews. Dr. Gordon Johnson, Provost of the Gates Cambridge Trust, has articulated this point via content on the Gates Website and through various NAFA communications. The following is lifted directly from "The Interview Process" on the Gates Cambridge Web site, http://www.gatesscholar.org: "Candidates will be asked about their work: why it excites them; what they know about the broader field of which it is part; why it is important; why coming to Cambridge will help them with their research or build on their earlier educational experiences. Also, do they understand that higher education brings privilege and opens opportunity for the future; what do they intend to do with the benefits they've had; how do they see themselves contributing in time. Candidates may also be asked questions of a probing intellectual or ethical dimension, to which there are no 'right' answers."

3. Louis Blair, Executive Secretary Emeritus of the Truman Scholarship Foundation, has noted that he prefers candidates who appear a bit tense at the outset of an interview. For Mr. Blair, such nervousness reflects that the student is taking the experience seriously. However, from an interviewee's perspective, the ability to relax and answer questions in a dynamic manner is equally crucial.

4. From "The Ideal Candidate," on the Gates Cambridge Web site, http://www.gatesscholar.org.

Chapter Ten: Involving Faculty in the Scholarship Process

1. Special thanks go to Amy Eckhardt, University of Pittsburgh; Carolyn Emigh, Georgetown University; and Lisa Grimes, College of William and Mary, co-presenters on the panel *Models of Faculty Involvement in the Scholarship Process* at the NAFA conference in Washington, DC.

Chapter Eleven: Undergraduate Research Revisited: Resources for Faculty and Opportunities for Students

1. For more detailed information visit the CUR Web site: http://www.cur.org/.

2. Previously the Reinvention Center's home was the State University of New York, Stony Brook (from circa 2002–2006).

3. See http://naples.cc.sunysb.edu/Pres/boyer.nsf.

4. For more information visit their Web site: http://www.reinventioncenter.miami.edu/.

5. For more information please visit the Web site: http://www.nchchonors.org/.

6. http://www.nasa.gov/audience/forstudents/postsecondary/learning/Undergraduate_Student.html

7. A partnership with the Department of Defense supports REU Sites in DoD-relevant research areas.

8. For a complete listing visit the NSF Web site: http://www.nsf.gov/crssprgm/reu/reu_search.cfm.

9. For more information on both programs visit the NIH Web site: http://www.training.nih.gov/student/sip/index.asp.

10. For more information visit the NIST Web site: http://www.surf.nist.gov/surf2.htm.

11. See the Department of Energy Web site: http://www.scied.science.doe.gov/scied/ERULF/about.html.

12. For more information visit the NCUR Web site: http://www.ncur.org/.

13. For more information visit the CUR Posters on the Hill Web site: http://www.cur.org/postersession.html.

Appendices: Competitive Scholarships, Opportunities, and Internships at a Glance

1. This list was compiled by Kathleen Cargill, who has served as the Director of the McNair Scholars Program at the College of St. Scholastica in Duluth, Minnesota, for ten years. She is a Fellow of the Society for Applied Anthropology and a member of the Minnesota College Personnel Association, the American Association of University Women, the MN ACE Network, and NAFA.

Appendices

NAFA Foundation and Institutional Membership

EXECUTIVE BOARD OF DIRECTORS:

Paula Warrick, President, American University
Jane Morris, Vice President, Villanova University
John Richardson, Treasurer, University of Louisville
Mona Pitre-Collins, Secretary, University of Washington
Tara Yglesias, Foundation Liaison, Truman Scholarship Foundation

BOARD MEMBERS:

John Bader, Johns Hopkins University
Joanne Brzinski, Emory University
Doug Cutchins, Grinnell College
Amy Eckhardt, University of Pittsburg
Beth Fiori, Cornell University
Paula Goldsmid, Pomona College
Scott Henderson, Furman College
Ruth Ost, Temple University
Linna Place, University of Missouri-Kansas City
Margaret Tongue, Union College
Alex Trayford, Wheaton College

FOUNDATION MEMBERS:

American-Scandinavian Foundation
Beinecke Scholarship Program
DC Department of Human Resources
Flinn Foundation
Foundation for Educational Exchange Between Canada and the U.S.
Gates Cambridge Trust
Jack Kent Cooke Foundation
James Madison Memorial Fellowship Foundation
Knowles Science and Teaching Foundation
Krell Institute
Marshall Scholarships
Morris K. Udall Foundation
National Science Foundation
NSEP David L. Boren Graduate Fellowships
Paul & Daisy Soros Foundation
Rhodes Scholarship Trust
Rotary Foundation of Rotary International
SCIO (Scholarship & Christianity in Oxford)
Steamboat Foundation
Truman Scholarship Foundation
United Negro College Fund Special Programs Corporation
Washington Center for Internships and Academic Seminars
Winston Churchill Foundation
Woodrow Wilson National Fellowship Foundation

INSTITUTIONAL MEMBERS:

Abilene Christian University
Alma College
American University
Amherst College
Appalachian State University
Arizona State University
Augsburg College
Austin College
Ball State University

Bard College
Barnard College
Bates College
Baylor University
Bennington College
Berry College
Binghamton University
Bowdoin College
Brandeis University

Brigham Young University
Brown University
Bryn Mawr College
Butler University
California Institute of Technology
California State Polytechnic
  University, Pomona
Carnegie Mellon University
Chapman University
Christopher Newport University
City College of New York
Claremont McKenna College
Clarion University of
  Pennsylvania
Clark University
Clemson University
Colgate University
College of Charleston
College of New Jersey
College of Staten Island
College of St. Benedict / St.
  John's University
College of St. Scholastica
College of the Holy Crosse
College of William & Mary
Colorado School of Mines
Colorado State University
Columbia College
Columbia University
Concordia College
Connecticut College
Corcoran College of Art and
  Design
Cornell University
CUNY Brooklyn College
Dartmouth College
Denison University

DePauw University
Dickinson College
Doane College
Drexel University
Duke University
Eastern Illinois University
Elmhurst College
Elmira College
Elon University
Emory University
Fairmont State College
Florida International University
Florida State University
Fordham University
Fort Hays State University
Furman University
George Fox University
George Mason University
George Washington University
Georgetown University
Georgia Institute of Technology
Georgia Southern University
Gettysburg College
Grand Valley State University
Grinnell College
Hamilton College
Harding University
Harvard University
Hendrix College
Hobart & William Smith Colleges
Hofstra University
Holy Family University
Illinois State University
Indiana University
Indiana University of PA
Iowa State University
James Madison University

John Brown University
John Carroll University
Johns Hopkins University
Juniata College
Kalamazoo College
Kansas State University
Kennesaw State University
Kent State University,
    Stark Campus
Kentucky State University
Lafayette College
Lebanon Valley College
Lehigh University
Linfield College
Louisiana State University
Loyola College in Maryland
Loyola Marymount University
Lynchburg College
Manhattan College
Marist College
Maryland Institute College of Art
Massachusetts Institute of
    Technology
Messiah College
Miami University of Ohio
Michigan State University
Middlesex Community College
Middle Tennessee State University
Middlebury College
Mississippi State University
Missouri State University
Mount Holyoke College
Muhlenberg College
Murray State University
New College of Florida
New England Conservatory
New Mexico State University

New York Stem School of
    Business
New York University
North Carolina Central University
North Carolina State University
Northwestern State University
Northwestern University
Nova Southeastern University
Oak Ridge Associated Universities
Oberlin College
Occidental College
Ohio Northern University
Ohio State University
Ohio University
Ohio Wesleyan University
Oklahoma City University
Oklahoma State University
Oral Roberts University
Oregon State University
Pennsylvania State—Behrend
Pennsylvania State University
Pepperdine University
Philadelphia University
Pitzer College
Point Loma Nazarene University
Pomona College
Princeton University
Purdue University
Queens College
Radford University
Reed College
Rice University
RIT - College of Liberal Arts
Rollins College
Roosevelt University
San Diego State University
San Francisco State University

Santa Clara University
Seton Hall University
Simmons College
Skidmore College
Smith College
South Dakota State University
Southern Illinois University,
    Carbondale
Southwestern University
Stephens Institute of Technology
St. Anselm College
St. John's College, Annapolis
St. John's College, Santa Fe
St. Joseph's University
St. Louis University
Stanford University
SUNY at Buffalo
SUNY Cortland
SUNY Potsdam
Swarthmore College
Syracuse University
Temple University
Tennessee Technological
    University
Texas A&M University
Texas Tech University
Texas Women's University
The Citadel
Trinity College
Truman State University
Tulane University
Union College
United States Air Force Academy
United States Coast Guard
    Academy
United States Military Academy
University of Akron

University of Alabama
University of Alabama at
    Birmingham
University of Arizona
University of Arkansas
University of Arkansas at
    Little Rock
University of California, Berkeley
University of California, Davis
University of California, Irvine
University of California,
    Los Angeles
University of California, Merced
University of California, Riverside
University of Central Arkansas
University of Central Florida
University of Cincinnati
University of Colorado at Boulder
University of Connecticut
University of Dayton
University of Delaware
University of Denver
University of Florida
University of Georgia
University of Houston
University of Illinois at Chicago
University of Illinois at
    Urbana-Champaign
University of Iowa
University of Kansas
University of Kentucky
University of Maryland, Baltimore
    County
University of Maryland,
    College Park
University of Massachusetts
    Amherst

University of Memphis
University of Miami
University of Michigan,
Ann Arbor
University of Minnesota, Morris
University of Minnesota,
Twin Cities
University of Mississippi
University of Missouri - Columbia
University of Missouri -
Kansas City
University of Montana
University of Nebraska - Lincoln
University of Nevada, Las Vegas
University of Nevada, Reno
University of New Hampshire
University of North Carolina at
Chapel Hill
University of North Carolina at
Greensboro
University of North Carolina at
Wilmington
University of North Dakota
University of North Florida
University of North Texas
University of Notre Dame
University of Oklahoma
University of Ottawa
University of the Pacific
University of Pennsylvania
University of Pittsburgh
University of Portland
University of Puget Sound
University of Rhode Island
University of Rochester
University of San Diego
University of Scranton

University of South Carolina
University of South Dakota
University of South Florida
University of Southern Mississippi
University of Tennessee
University of Texas at Austin
University of Texas at Dallas
University of Tulsa
University of Utah
University of Vermont
University of Virginia
University of Washington
University of Wisconsin –
Eau Claire
University of Wisconsin –
Madison
University of Wyoming
Ursinus College
Utah State University
Valdosta State University
Valparaiso University
Vanderbilt University
Vassar College
Villanova University
Virginia Commonwealth
University
Virginia Military Institute
Virginia Tech University
Wake Forest University
Washington and Lee University
Washington State University
Wayne State University
Wellesley College
Wesleyan University
West Texas A&M University
West Virginia University
Western Carolina University

Western Kentucky University
Western Washington University
Westminster College
Wheaton College (MA)
Whitman College
Willamette University
William Jewel College

Williams College
Winthrop University
Worcester Polytechnic Institute
Wright State University
Yale University
Yeshiva University

Competitive Scholarships and Internships at a Glance[1]

AACN

Eligible	Nursing majors
Eligible	All colleges and uiversities in the United States
Host Institution	American Association of Critical-Care Nurses (AACN)
App Deadline	Early May
Contact	Educational Advancement Scholarships/American Association of Critical Care Nurses (AACN)/101 Columbia/Aliso Virn, CA 92656-1491/Tel: 800-899-2226, ext. 376 http://www.campusrn.com/scholarships/scholarship_detail.asp?scholarship_id=123&browse=A

AGHE AARP Andrus Foundation Founder's Scholar Campaign

Eligible	Undergraduates
Eligible	All colleges and universities
Host Institution	Association for Gerontology in Higher Education
App Deadline	Variable deadlines
Contact	Association for Gerontology in Higher Education/ 1030 15th Street, NW, Suite 240 / Washington, DC 20005/ Tel: 202-289-9806 / Fax: 202) 289-9824 http://www.aghe.org/templates/System/default.asp?id=40634

AT&T Undergraduate Research Program

Eligible	Members of a minority group underrepresented in the sciences; for example, women, African Americans, Hispanics, or Native Americans
Eligible	All Colleges and Universities
Host Institution	AT&T
App Deadline	Late January
Contact	AT&T Labs URPA / Room D32-A04 / 200 Laurel Ave. / Middletown, NJ 07748 http://www.research.att.com/internships

Austrian Teaching Assistantship Program

Eligible	Prospective English teachers who are fluent in German
Eligible	All colleges and universities
Host Institution	Austrian Ministry of Education, Science and Culture (Austrian Gov/Embassy)
App Deadline	Mid-February
Contact	Austrian-American Educational Commission, quartier2l / MQ / Museumsplatz 1 / A-1070 Wien / Austria / Europe / Tel: +43-1-236 7878 0 / Fax: +43-1-236 7878 17 http://www.fulbright.at/us_citizens/ teaching_intro.php

Ayn Rand Essay Scholarships

Eligible	College students
Eligible	All colleges and universities
Host Institution	Ayn Rand Institute
App Deadline	Mid-September
Contact	Atlas Shrugged Essay Contest / Dept. W / The Ayn Rand Institute / PO Box 57044 / Irvine, CA 92691-7044 http://www.aynrand.org/site/ PageServer?pagename=education_contests_atlas

Bill Emerson National Hunger Fellowship

Eligible	Graduating seniors and recent graduates
Eligible	All colleges and universities
Host Institution	Emerson Selection Committee, Congressional Hunger Center
App Deadline	Mid-January
Contact	Emerson Selection Committee / Congressional Hunger Center / 229-1/2 Pennsylvania Ave. SE / Washington, DC 20003 / fax: 202-547-7575 / fellows@hungercenter.org http://servicelearning.org/resources/ funding_sources/index.php?popup_id=720

Breakthrough Collaborative (Formerly Known as Summerbridge)

Eligible	Prospective teachers
Eligible	All colleges and universities
Host Institution	The Breakthrough Collaborative
App Deadline	Early March
Contact	Breakthrough Collaborative / 40 First Street, 5th Floor / San Francisco, CA 94105 / Tel: 415-442-0600 / Fax: 415-442-0609 / info@breakthroughcollaborative.org http://www.summerbridge.org/

Center for Urban Redevelopment Excellence

Eligible	Promising young professionals
Eligible	All colleges and universities
Host Institution	University of Pennsylvania
App Deadline	Multiple deadlines exist. See Web site for details
Contact	ATTN: Fellowship Applications / Center for Urban Redevelopment Excellence / PennDesign/Meyerson Hall / University of Pennsylvania / 210 South 34th Street / Philadelphia, PA 19104-6311 / Tel: 215-898-4653 / rockfell@design.upenn.edu http://www.upenn.edu/curexpenn/program.htm

Charles B. Rangel International Affairs Fellowship Program

Eligible	Students interested in pursuing a career in the Foreign Service of the U.S. Dept. of State
Eligible	All colleges and universities
Host Institution	Ralph J. Bunche International Affairs Center
App Deadline	Late January
Contact	Dr. Carole Henderson Tyson, Program Manager / Charles B. Rangel, International Affairs Program / Ralph J. Bunche, International Affairs Center / Howard University / 2218 6th Street NW / Washington, DC 20059 / Tel: 202-806-4367 / Fax: 202-387-6951 / chtyson@howard.edu www.howard.edu/rjb/rangelprogram.htm

City Year

Eligible	Young adults, ages 17 to 24, from diverse racial, cultural, and socioeconomic backgrounds
Eligible	All colleges and universities
Host Institution	AmeriCorps
App Deadline	Rolling basis
Contact	City Year Headquarters / 287 Columbus Ave. / Boston, MA 02116 / Tel: 617-927-2500 / Fax: 617-927-2510 www.cityyear.org

Community Fellows Program

Eligible	Recent college graduates
Eligible	All colleges and universities
Host Institution	United Way of America
App Deadline	See Web site for details
Contact	United Way of America / 701 N. Fairfax Street / Alexandra, VA 22314 http://national.unitedway.org/jobs/fellows.cfm

Community Intern Program

Eligible	All students
Eligible	All colleges and universities
Host Institution	U.S. Environmental Protection Agency (EPA)
App Deadline	Late January
Contact	Environmental Careers Organization / Attention: Community Intern Program / 30 Winter Street, Sixth Floor / Boston, MA 02108 / Tel: 617-426-4783, ext. 147 / Liz Cavano, Intern Coordinator for ECO / http://www.epa.gov/compliance/ environmentaljustice/interns/index

Coro Fellows Program in Public Affairs

Eligible	Graduates with civic experience
Eligible	All colleges and universities
Host Institution	CORO
App Deadline	Early January
Contact	Coro Northern California Office / 580 California Street, 7th Floor / San Francisco, CA 94104 / Tel: 415-986-0521, ext. 222 http://www.coro.org/programs/ fellows_program/fellows_program.h

DAAD—German Academic Exchange Service Graduate Scholarship

Eligible	Graduating seniors and graduate students of all disciplines wishing to study in Germany or complete a postgraduate or Master's degree course and obtain a degree from a German higher education institution
Eligible	All colleges and universities
Host Institution	DAAD
App Deadline	Early October to Late July

Contact   DAAD New York Office / 871 United Nations
                 Plaza / New York, NT 10017 / Tel: 212-758-3223 /
                 Fax: 212-755-5780 / daadny@daad.org
                 http://www.daad.org/?p=gradstudy

DAAD—German Academic Exchange Service Undergraduate Scholarship

Eligible   Undergraduates who are interested in studying in
                  Germany
Eligible   All colleges and universities
Host Institution DAAD
App Deadline   Varies
Contact   DAAD New York Office / 871 United Nations
                  Plaza / New York, NT 10017 / Tel: 212-758-3223 /
                  Fax: 212-755-5780 / daadny@daad.org
                  http://www.daad.org/?p=50407

Department of Health and Human Services Emerging Leaders Program

Eligible   Undergraduate and graduate students
Eligible   All colleges and universities
Host Institution Department of Health and Human Services
App Deadline   Mid-March
Contact   The U.S. Department of Health and Human
                  Services / 200 Independence Ave. SW /
                  Washington, DC 20201 / Tel: 202-619-0257 /
                  Toll Free: 1-877-696-6775
                  http://hhsu.learning.hhs.gov/elp/

Department of Homeland Security Graduate & Undergraduate Fellowship Program

Eligible   Students interested in pursuing the basic science
                  and technology innovations that can be applied to
                  the DHS mission

Eligible   All colleges and universities
Host Institution   Oak Ridge Institute for Science and Education
                      DHS Scholarship and
                      Fellowship Program
App Deadline   Late January
Contact   Oak Ridge Institute for Science and Education
                      DHS Scholarship and Fellowship Program /
                      PO Box 117 MS 36 / Oak Ridge, TN 37831-0117 /
                      Tel: 206-221-6023 / dhsed@orau.gov
                      http://www.orau.gov/dhsed/Default.htm

Echoing Green Foundation Public Service Fellowships

Eligible   Emerging social entrepreneurs who plan to start up
                      and lead innovative, replicable, and sustainable
                      public service projects
Eligible   All colleges and universities
Host Institution   Echoing Green
App Deadline   See Web site for multiple deadlines
Contact   Echoing Green / 494 Eighth Ave., 2nd Floor /
                      Tel: 212-689-1165 / Fax: 212-689-9010 /
                      info@echoinggreen.org
                      http://www.echoinggreen.org/
                      index.cfm?fuseaction=Page.viewPage&pageId=41

Elie Wiesel Prize for Humanity

Eligible   Undergraduates
Eligible   All colleges and universities
Host Institution   Elie Wiesel Foundation
App Deadline   December
Contact   The Elie Wiesel Foundation for Humanity /
                      555 Madison Avenue / 20th Floor /
                      New York, NY 10022 /
                      Fax: 212-490-6006
                      http://www.eliewieselfoundation.org/

Environmental Leadership Training Program

Eligible	Environmental policy advocates
Eligible	All colleges and universities
Host Institution	Green Corps
App Deadline	Mid-November
Contact	Green Corps / ATTN: Jesse Littlewood / 44 Winter Street, 4th Floor / Boston, MA 02108 / Tel: 617-426-8506 / Fax: 617-292-8057 / jobs@greencorps.org http://www.greencorps.org/training.asp?id2=19458

Environmental Protection Agency Greater Research Opportunities Fellowships for Undergraduate and Graduate Students

Eligible	Sophomore and senior undergraduates and graduate students
Eligible	All colleges and universities
Host Institution	Environmental Protection Agency
App Deadline	Varies by scholarship and fellowship
Contact	Bronda Harrison, U.S. Environmental Protection Agency /Ariel Rios Building / 1200Pennsylvania Avenue NW / Washington, DC 20460 / Tel: 202-343-9777 http://es.epa.gov/ncer/rfa/2007/ 2007_star_gro_undergrad.html

Environmental Protection Agency Science to Achieve Results Fellowships

Eligible	Sophomore and senior undergraduates and graduate students
Eligible	All colleges and universities
Host Institution	Environmental Protection Agency
App Deadline	Varies by scholarship and fellowship
Contact	U.S. Environmental Protection Agency / Ariel Rios Building / 1200 Pennsylvania Avenue NW /

Washington, DC 20460
http://es.epa.gov/ncer/rfa/
2007/2007_star_fellow.html

Everett Public Service Internship Program

Eligible   Undergraduate and graduate students
Eligible   All colleges and universities
Host Institution   Everett Public Research Internship Program
App Deadline   Late August
Contact   Samantha Saanon / The Everett Public Service
Internship Program / c/o Co-op America / 1612 K
Street NW, Suite 600 / Washington, DC 20006 /
everettinternships@coopamerica.org
http://www.everettinternships.org/
apply/index.html

FBI Honors Internship Program

Eligible   All students with a minimum 3.0/4 GPA
Eligible   All colleges and universities
Host Institution   Federal Bureau of Investigation
App Deadline   Early October
Contact   Washington Metropolitan Field Office / 601 4th
Street NW / Washington, DC 20535-0002 / Tel:
202-278-2000 / washingtondc.fbi.gov
http://www.fbijobs.gov/231.asp

Freeman Peace Internships

Eligible   People between the ages of 19 and 26
Eligible   All colleges and universities
Host Institution   Fellowship of Reconciliation (FOR)
App Deadline   Late May
Contact   Maryrose Dolezal / 1050 Selby Ave. / St. Paul,
MN 55104
http://www.forusa.org/programs/internships.html

Freeman-ASIA Awards for Study in Asia

Eligible	American undergraduates with demonstrated financial need who are planning to study overseas in East or Southeast Asia
Eligible	All colleges and universities
Host Institution	U.S. Student Programs Division Institute of International Education
App Deadline	See Web site for multiple deadlines
Contact	U.S. Student Programs Division / Institute of International / 809 United Nations Plaza, New York, NY 10017-3580 / Tel: 212-984-5542 / Fax: 212-984-5325 / freeman-ASIA@iie.org http://www.iie.org/programs/freeman-asia/

Ernest F. Hollings Undergraduate Scholarship Program

Eligible	College juniors
Eligible	All colleges and universities
Host Institution	National Oceanic and Atmospheric Administration (NOAA), a federal science agency in the Department of Commerce
App Deadline	Early February
Contact	NOOA / 14th Street and Constitution Avenue NW, Room 6217 / Washington, DC 20230 / Tel: 202-482-6090 / Fax: 202-482-3154 / StudentScholarshipPrograms@noaa.gov http://www.oesd.noaa.gov/Hollings_info.html

Frances Tompkins Nursing

Eligible	All students currently enrolled in state-approved schools of nursing or pre-nursing in associated degree, baccalaureate, diploma, generic doctorate, and generic master's programs
Eligible	All colleges and universities

Host Institution	National Student Nurses Association
App Deadline	Early January
Contact	NSNA / 45 Main Street, Suite 606 / Brooklyn, NY 11201 / Tel: 718-210-0710 / Fax: 718-210-0710 / nana@nsna.org www.nsna.org

Fulbright Grant

Eligible	Students interested in graduate study abroad
Eligible	All colleges and universities
Host Institution	Institute of International Education
App Deadline	Mid-October
Contact	Walter Jackson, Program Manager / Tel: 212-984-5327 / wjackson@iie.org http://www.iie.org/fulbright/

Future Leaders Fellows Program

Eligible	Students with leadership qualities, international experiences and perspectives, strong academics, proficiency in a foreign language, and strong communication skills
Eligible	All colleges and universities
Host Institution	The Population Institute
App Deadline	Mid-April
Contact	Sujata Chakraborty / Department: HR / Tel: 202-544-3300 / Fax: 202-544-0068 / sujata@populationinstitute.org http://www.populationinstitute.org/careers/index.php?detail&lid=4

Gates Cambridge Scholarship

Eligible	Students interested in graduate study at Cambridge

Eligible	All colleges and universities
Host Institution	University of Cambridge
App Deadline	Mid-October
Contact	Gates Cambridge Trust / PO Box 252 / Cambridge CB2 1TZ England / info@gates.scholarships.cam.ac.uk http://www.gates.scholarships.cam.ac.uk/

George Aratani / Daniel K. Inouye Fellowship

Eligible	Graduate students who have a commitment to the Asian American and Pacific Islander communities and who plan to pursue a public policy career
Eligible	All colleges and universities
Host Institution	Asian Pacific American Institute for Congressional Studies (APAICS)
App Deadline	Late February
Contact	APAICS: 2007/2008 Fellowship Programs / 1001 Connecticut Avenue NW / Washington, DC 20036 / Tel: 202-296-9200 / apaics@apaics.org http://www.apaics.org/apaics_fellow.html

George J. Mitchell Scholarship

Eligible	Students interested in graduate study in Ireland
Eligible	All colleges and universities
Host Institution	U.S.-Ireland Alliance
App Deadline	Early October
Contact	U.S.-Ireland Alliance / Mary Lou Hartman, Director of George Mitchell Scholarship Program / 2800 Claredon Blvd. #502 West / Arlington, VA 22201 / Tel: 703-841-5843 / hartman@us-irelandalliance.org http://www.us-irelandalliance.org/ wmspage.cfm?parm1=34

Golden Key International Honour Society Scholarships

Eligible	Undergraduates
Eligible	See directory at: http://www.goldenkey.org/goldenkey/ gkfms/chapters/default.aspx
Host Institution	Golden Key International Honour Society
App Deadline	Varies by scholarship
Contact	Golden Key International Honour Society / 621 North Ave. NE, Suite C-100 / Atlanta, GA 30308 / Toll Free: 800-377-2401 / Tel: 404-377-2400 / Fax. 678-420-6757 / awards@goldenkey.org http://www.goldenkey.org/GKweb/ ScholarshipsandAwards/

Goldwater Scholarship and Excellence in Education Program

Eligible	Sophomores and juniors with a desire to pursue an advanced degree in mathematics, science, or engineering (applicants must be nominated by an institutional representative)
Eligible	See Web site
Host Institution	The Barry M. Goldwater Scholarship Foundation
App Deadline	Early February
Contact	Barry M. Goldwater Scholarship and Excellence in Education Foundation / 6225 Brandon Avenue, Suite 315 / Springfield, VA 22150-2519 / Tel: 703-756-6012 / Fax: 702-756-6015 / goldh2o@vacoxmail.com http://www.act.org/goldwater/

Graduate Partnerships Program

Eligible	Medical students
Eligible	All colleges and universities
Host Institution	National Institutes of Health

App Deadline	Varies by program
Contact	Graduate Partnerships Program / National Institutes of Health—DHHA / 2 Center Drive: Building 2 / Room 2E06 / Bethesda, MD 20892-0234 / Tel: 301-594-9605 / Fax: 301-594-9606 / gpp@nih.gov http://gpp.nih.gov/

Graduate Research Fellowship Program

Eligible	Graduate students
Eligible	All colleges and universities
Host Institution	National Science Foundation
App Deadline	Varies by discipline
Contact	The National Science Foundation / 4201 Wilson Boulevard / Arlington, VA 22230 / Tel: 202-331-3542 / help@nsfgradfellows.org http://www.nsf.gov/funding/ pgm_summ.isp?pims_id=6201

GrantsNet

Eligible	Undergraduate, graduate, medical students, postdocs, and faculty-varies by program
Eligible	Varies by program
Host Institution	American Association for the Advancement of Science
App Deadline	Varies by program
Contact	Science / AAAS / 1200 New York Avenue NW / Washington, DC 20005 / Tel: 202-326-6550 http://sciencecareers.sciencemag.org/funding

Harry S. Truman Scholarship

Eligible	College juniors interested in pursing a career in public service (applicants must be nominated by institutional representative)

Eligible   See Web site
Host Institution   Harry S. Truman Scholarship Foundation
App Deadline   Early February
Contact   Harry S. Truman Scholarship Foundation /
                      712 Jackson Place NW / Washington, DC 20006 /
                      Tel: 202-395-4831 / Fax: 202-395-6995 /
                      office@truman.gov
                      http://www.truman.gov/candidates/candidates.htm

Herbert Scoville Jr. Peace Fellowship

Eligible   College graduates
Eligible   All colleges and universities
Host Institution   Herbert Scoville Jr. Peace Fellowship
App Deadline   Early February
Contact   Paul Revsine, Program Director / Herbert Scoville
                      Jr. Peace Fellowships / 322 4th Street NE /
                      Washington, DC 20002
                      http://www.scoville.org/

Hertz Foundation Graduate Fellowships

Eligible   PhD candidates in the applied physical and
                      engineering sciences, as well as those areas in
                      modern biology that apply the physical sciences
                      intensively
Eligible   See Web site
Host Institution   The Hertz Foundation
App Deadline   Early April
Contact   Fannie and John Hertz Foundation /
                      2456 Research Drive / Livermore,
                      CA 94550-3850 / Tel: 925-373-1642 /
                      Fax: 925-373-6329 /
                      askhertz@hertzfoundation.org
                      http://www.hertzfndn.org/dx/Fellowships/

Hispanic Scholarship Fund Scholarships

Eligible	All students
Eligible	Varies by program
Host Institution	Hispanic Scholarship Fund
App Deadline	Varies by scholarship
Contact	Hispanic Scholarship Fund, Headquarters / 55 Second Street, Suite 1500 / San Francisco, CA 94105 / Tel: 1-887-473-4636 / Fax: 415-808-2302 / scholar1@hsf.net http://www.hsf.net/

Historic Preservation Internship Training Program

Eligible	All students
Eligible	All colleges and universities
Host Institution	National Park Service, U.S. Department of the Interior
App Deadline	Mid-February
Contact	National Council for Preservation Education / ATTN: Michael A. Tomlan / 210 West Sibley Hall / Cornell University / Ithaca, NY http://www.nps.gov/hps/tps/intern/internships.htm

Homeland Security Undergraduate Scholarships for Rising Juniors

Eligible	Undergraduates with a cumulative GPA of 3.3 or higher
Eligible	All colleges and universities
Host Institution	U.S. Department of Homeland Security Science & Technology Directorate, Office of Research & Development, University Programs
App Deadline	Late January
Contact	Oak Ridge Institute for Science and Education DHS Scholarship and Fellowship Program / PO Box 117 MS 36 / Oak Ridge, TN 37831-0117 /

dhsed@orau.gov / Tel: 206-221-6023
http://www.orau.gov/dhsed/

Humanity in Action Internships

Eligible	Varies by internship
Eligible	All colleges and universities
Host Institution	Humanity in Action
App Deadline	Varies by internship
Contact	Nicholas M. Farrell / American Program Coordinator / 25 WashingtonStreet, 4th Floor / Brooklyn, NY 11201 / Tel: 718-237-5774 / Fax: 718-237-6264 http://www.humanityinaction.org/

Indian Health Service Scholarships

Eligible	Students intending to become health professionals serving Native American communities
Eligible	All colleges and universities
Host Institution	Indian Health Service
App Deadline	Late February
Contact	Indian Health Service / Scholarship Program / 801 Thompson Avenue, Suite 120 / Rockville, MD 20852 / Tel: 301-443-6197 / Fax: 301-443-6048 http://www.ihs.gov/JobsCareerDevelop/ DHPS/Scholarships/Scholarship_index.asp

Institute for International Public Policy Undergraduate Fellowships

Eligible	College sophomores
Eligible	All colleges and universities
Host Institution	Institute for International Public Policy
App Deadline	Mid-March
Contact	Institute for International Public Policy / 2750 Prosperity Avenue, Suite 600 / Fairfax, VA 22031 /

Tel: 703-205-7624 / Toll Free: 1-800-530-6232 /
Fax: 703-205-7645 / fafadmin@woodrow.org
http://www.uncfsp.org/iipp/content/program.cfm

Institute on Philanthropy and Voluntary Service

Eligible   Undergraduates
Eligible   All colleges and universities
Host Institution   The Fund for American Studies and the Center of
                    Philanthropy at Indiana University
App Deadline   December
Contact   The Center on Philanthropy at Indiana University /
                    550 West North Street, Suite 301 / Indianapolis,
                    IN 46202 / Tel: 317-274-4300 /
                    Fax: 317-684-8900 / Marsha Currin at
                    mcurrin@iupui.edu
                    http://www.philanthropy.iupui.edu/
                    Education/Institute.aspx

International Institute for Political and Economic Studies

Eligible   All students
Eligible   All colleges and universities
Host Institution   The Fund for American Studies (TFAS)
                    International
App Deadline   Late January
Contact   International Institute for Political and Economic
                    Studies / The Fund for American Studies / 1706
                    New Hampshire Avenue NW /
                    Washington, DC 20009 / Tel: 001-202-986-0384 /
                    Fax: 001-202--315-3880
                    http://www.tfasinternational.org/iipes/about/

Jack Kent Cooke Scholarship Program

Eligible   Graduating seniors and graduate students
                    (applicants must be nominated by institutional
                    representative)

Eligible	See Web site
Host Institution	Jack Kent Cooke Foundation
App Deadline	Mid-March
Contact	Jack Kent Cooke Foundation / 44325 Woodridge Parkway / Lansdowne, VA 20176 / Tel: 703-723-8000 / Fax: 703-723-8030 http://www.jkcf.org/

Jacob K. Javits Fellowship Program

Eligible	Prospective graduate and PhD students
Eligible	All colleges and universities
Host Institution	U.S. Department of Education
App Deadline	Early October
Contact	Carmen Gordon and Lakisha Reid / U.S. DoE, OPE, Teacher & Student Development Programs Service / Jacob K. Javits Fellowship Program / 1990 K Street NW, 6th Floor / Washington, DC 20006-8524 / Tel: 202-502-7542 / ope_javits_program@ed.gov http://www.ed.gov/programs/ iegpsjavits/index.html

James Madison Graduate Fellowships

Eligible	Graduating seniors interested in teaching history or a social science for the junior fellowships and current history or social science teachers for the senior awards
Eligible	All colleges and universities
Host Institution	James Madison Memorial Fellowship Foundation
App Deadline	Early March
Contact	James Madison Memorial Fellowship Foundation / 200 K Street NW, Suite 303 / Washington, DC 20006 / Tel: 202-653-8700 / Fax: 202-653-6045 / madison@act.org http://www.jamesmadison.com/index.html

Japan Exchange and Teaching (JET) Programme

Eligible	All students
Eligible	All colleges and universities
Host Institution	The Japan Exchange and Teaching Program
App Deadline	Varies by country
Contact	Council of Local Authorities for International Relations (CLAIR) / New York Office: Japan Local Government Center (CLAIR, New York) / 666 Fifth Avenue, 2nd Floor / New York, NY 10103-0072 / Tel: 212-246-5542 / Fax: 212-246-5617 http://www.jetprogramme.org/e/intro.html

Japanese Government (Monbukagakusho) Scholarships

Eligible	All students
Eligible	Scholarship recipients are recruited and initially screened by a Japanese embassy or consulate general
Host Institution	The Japanese Embassy
App Deadline	See Web site for multiple deadlines
Contact	Embassy of Japan in the United States / 2520 Massachusetts Avenue NW / Washington, DC 20008 / Main Tel: 202-238-6700 / Fax: 202-328-2187 / Visa Tel: 202-238-6800 / Fax: 202-328-2184 http://www.studyjapan.go.jp/en/toj/toj0302e.html

Killam Fellowships Program

Eligible	Undergraduates
Eligible	Limited to participating colleges and universities. See Web site for details
Host Institution	The Foundation for Educational Exchange Between Canada and theUnited States of America
App Deadline	Varies by institution

Contact   Ms. Michelle Emond / Program Officer for the
Killam Fellowships Program / Foundation for
Education Exchange Between Canada and
the United States of America / 350 Albert Street,
Suite 2015 / Ottawa, ON K1R 1A4 /
Tel: 613-688-5513 / Fax: 613-237-2029 /
memond@killamfellowships.com
http://www.killamfellowships.com

Knowles Math and Science Teaching Fellowship Program

Eligible   Students who have received a bachelor's or
advanced degree in science, engineering, or
mathematics and are committed to teaching high
school science and/or mathematics in U.S. schools

Eligible   All colleges and universities

Host Institution   Knowles Science Teaching Foundation

App Deadline   Mid-January

Contact   Jennifer Mossgrove, EdD, Program Officer,
Mathematics / Roseanne Rostock, PhD, Program
Officer, Science / Tel: 856-608-0001 /
Fax: 856-608-0008 / info@kstf.org
http://www.kstf.org/
teaching_fellowships_home.aspx

La Unidad Latina Foundation Scholarship

Eligible   Hispanic undergraduate and graduate students

Eligible   All colleges and universities

Host Institution   La Unidad Latina Foundation

App Deadline   Mid-February

Contact   La Unidad Latina Foundation / 359 Prospect
Avenue / Brooklyn, NY 11215 /
foundationalaunidadlatina.org
http://foundation.launidadlatina.org/Apply.htm

Luce Scholars Program

Eligible	Students with a bachelor's degree for a wide range of fields have not had the opportunity to study in Asia
Eligible	Limited to participating colleges and universities. See Web site for details
Host Institution	The Henry Luce Foundation, Inc.
App Deadline	Early December
Contact	The Henry Luce Foundation, Inc. / 51 Madison Avenue, 30th Floor / New York, NY 10010 / Tel: 212-489-7700 / Fax: 212-581-9541 http://hluce.org/3scholfm.html

Marshall Scholarship

Eligible	Students who want to pursue graduate studies in the United Kingdom
Eligible	All colleges and universities (applicants must be endorsed by their home institutions)
Host Institution	Foreign and Commonwealth Office, The Marshall Aid Commemoration Commission, on behalf of the UK Government
App Deadline	Early October
Contact	The British Council, British Embassy / 3100 Massachusetts Avenue NW / Washington, DC 20008-3600 / Tel: 212-588-7844 / WashingtonDC@marshallscholarship.org http://www.marshallscholarship.org/index.html

Mental Health and Substance Abuse Services Fellowship

Eligible	Students pursuing doctoral degrees in psychology
Eligible	All universities with APA-accredited doctoral programs
Host Institution	American Psychological Association
App Deadline	Mid-January

Contact	APA/MFP / MHSAS Application / 750 First Street NE / Washington, DC 20002-4242 / Tel: 202-336-6127 / Fax: 202-336-6012 / mfp@apa.org http://www.apa.org/mfp/postdocpsych.html

Merage Institute Fellows Program

Eligible	First-generation immigrant students
Eligible	Limited to Merage American partner universities. See Web site for details
Host Institution	Merage Foundation for the American Dream
App Deadline	Mid-December
Contact	Merage Foundations / 4350 Von Karman Avenue, Fourth Floor / Newport Beach, CA 92660 / Tel: 949-474-5880 / Fax: 949-474-5811 http://www.meragefoundations.com/ mfad_fellows.html

Midwest Student Exchange Program

Eligible	Students attending particular colleges and universities in Illinois, Indiana, Kansas, Michigan, Minnesota, Missouri, Nebraska, North Dakota, Ohio, South Dakota and Wisconsin
Eligible	See Web site
Host Institution	Midwestern Higher Education Compact
App Deadline	Varies by institute
Contact	MHEC / 1300 South Second St., Suite 130 / Minneapolis, MN 55454-1079 / Tel: 612-626-8288 / Fax: 612-626-8290 http://www.mhec.org/index.asp?pageid=1

Mississippi Teacher Corps

Eligible	College graduates
Eligible	All colleges and universities

Host Institution	The Mississippi Teacher Corps
App Deadline	See Web site for multiple deadlines
Contact	Mississippi Teacher Corps / School of Education, University of Mississippi / P O Box 1848 / University, MS 38677-1848 / Tel: 662-915-5224 / Fax: 622-915-7249 / mtc@olemiss.edu http://www.olemiss.edu/programs/mtc/

Morris K. Udall Native American Congressional Internship

Eligible	Juniors, seniors, and recent college graduates who are Native American
Eligible	All colleges and universities
Host Institution	Morris K. Udall Foundation
App Deadline	Late January
Contact	Morris K. Udall Foundation / 130 South Scott Avenue / Tucson, AZ 85701-1922 / Tel: 520-901-8500 / Fax: 520-670-5530 / info@udall.gov http://www.udall.gov/udall.asp?link=300

Morris K. Udall Scholarship

Eligible	Sophomores and juniors
Eligible	All colleges and universities (applicants must be nominated by institutional representative)
Host Institution	Morris K. Udall Foundation
App Deadline	Early March
Contact	Morris K. Udall Foundation / 130 South Scott Avenue / Tucson, AZ 85701-1922 / Tel: 520-901-8500 / Fax: 520-670-5530 / info@udall.gov http://www.udall.gov/udall.asp?link=700

NAACP Scholarships

Eligible	Varies by scholarship
Eligible	All colleges and universities
Host Institution	NAACP
App Deadline	Varies by scholarship
Contact	The United Negro College Fund / Scholarships and Grants Administration / 8260 Willow Oaks Corporate Drive / Fairfax, VA 22031 / Tel: 703-205-3400 http://www.naacp.org/advocacy/education/

National Air and Space Museum Summer Internship

Eligible	All students
Eligible	All colleges and universities
Host Institution	Smithsonian National Air and Space Museum
App Deadline	Mid-February
Contact	Summer Internship Program / Coordinator of Student Programs / PO Box 37012 / National Air and Space Museum / Education Services, Unit P-700, MRC 305 / Washington, DC 70013-7017 http://www.nasm.si.edu/getinvolved/internfellow.cfm

National Defense Sciences and Engineering Graduate Fellowship

Eligible	Graduating senior or graduate students
Eligible	All colleges and universities
Host Institution	Department of Defense
App Deadline	Early January
Contact	NDSEG Fellowship Program / c/o American Society for Engineering Education / 1818 N. Street NW, #600 / Washington, DC 20036 / Tel:202-331-3516 / Fax: 202-265-8504 / ndseg@asee.org http://www.asee.org/ndseg/

National Gallery of Art Summer Internship

Eligible	Varies by program
Eligible	All colleges and universities
Host Institution	The National Gallery of Art
App Deadline	Information not yet available on Web site
Contact	The National Gallery of Art / 20008 South Club Drive / Landover, MD 20785 / Tel: 202-842-6257 / Fax: 202-842-6925 / intern@nga.gov http://www.nga.gov/education/internsumm.shtm

National Institutes of Health Undergraduate Scholarship Program

Eligible	Students from disadvantaged backgrounds who are committed to health-related careers in biomedical, behavioral, and social science
Eligible	All colleges and universities
Host Institution	National Institutes of Health
App Deadline	Late February
Contact	Undergraduate Scholarship Program / National Institutes of Health / 2 Center Drive, Room 2E24, MSC 0230 / Bethesda, MD 02892-0230 / Tel: 888-352-3001 / Fax: 301-480-3123 / ugsp@nih.gov http://www.ugsp.nih.gov/ overview_faqs/overview_faqs.asp?m=01&s

NSEP David L. Boren Graduate Fellowship

Eligible	U.S. citizens enrolled in or applying to a graduate degree program abroad. See Web site for eligible countries.
Eligible	All colleges and universities
Host Institution	The National Security Education Program
App Deadline	Late January
Contact	NSEP / David L. Boren Undergraduate Scholarships and Graduate

Fellowships / Institute of International Education /
1400 K Street NW, 6th Floor /Washington,
DC 20005-2403 / Tel: 1-800-618-NSEP /
Fax:202-326-7672 / nsep@iie.org
http://www.iie.org/programs/
nsep/graduate/default.htm

NSEP David L. Boren Undergraduate Scholarship

Eligible	Students looking for study abroad experience
Eligible	All colleges and universities
Host Institution	The National Security Education Program
App Deadline	Early February
Contact	NSEP / David L. Boren Undergraduate Scholarships and Graduate Fellowships / Institute of International Education / 1400 K Street NW, 6th Floor / Washington, DC 20005-2403 / Tel: 1-800-618-NSEP / Fax:202-326-7672 / nsep@iie.org http://www.iie.org/Template.cfm?&Template=/ programs/nsep/default

NSEP National Flagship Language Program Fellowship

Eligible	Graduating senior or graduate student
Eligible	All colleges and universities
Host Institution	Institute of International Education
App Deadline	Mid-January
Contact	NSEP, National Flagship Language Program / Institute of International Education / 1400 K Street NW, 6th Floor / Washington, DC 20005-2403 / Tel: 1-800-618-NSEP / Fax: 202-326-7672 http://www.iie.org/programs/ nsep/flagship/default.htm

Newton Fellowship Program

Eligible	Recent college graduates and mid-career professionals
Eligible	All colleges and universities
Host Institution	Math for America
App Deadline	Early February
Contact	Math for America / Church St. Station / PO Box 3448 / New York, NY 10008 / Tel: 212-206-0053 / Fax: 212-514-8269 / information@mathforamerica.org http://www.mathforamerica.org/ htdocs/template.php?section=apply&content=nf

NIST Scholarship for Service

Eligible	All students
Eligible	NIST's Office of Personnel Management selects colleges and universities that meet its federal criteria for this program. See Web site for details.
Host Institution	National Institute of Standards and Technology (NIST)
App Deadline	Late January
Contact	U.S. Office of Personnel Management / 1900 E. Street NW / Washington, DC 20415 / Tel: 202-606-1800 / TTY: 202-606-2532 http://www.nist.gov/

North American Language and Culture Assistants in Spain

Eligible	Prospective English teachers who are fluent in German
Eligible	All colleges and universities
Host Institution	The Ministry of Education and Science of Spain (MEC)
App Deadline	Mid-April

Contact	Language and Culture Assistant Program / Embassy of Spain /Education Office / 2375 Pennsylvania Ave. NW / Washington, DC 20037 / Tel: 202-728-2335 / Fax: 202-728-2313 http://www.mec.es/sgci/usa/en/ programs/us_assistants/default.shtml#guide

Organization of American States Program of Scholarships and Training

Eligible	Junior, senior, and graduate students
Eligible	All colleges and universities
Host Institution	Organization of American States (OAS)
App Deadline	Mid-April through June. see Web site for details
Contact	Educational Portal of the Americas / Department of Human Development / Organization of American States / 1889 F Street NW / Washington, DC 20006 / Tel: 202-458-6166 / scholarships@oas.org http://www.oas.org/EN/PINFO/HR/ gen_information.htm

Organization of American States Student Intern Program

Eligible	Varies by program
Eligible	All colleges and universities
Host Institution	Organization of American States (OAS)
App Deadline	Varies by country
Contact	Educational Portal of the Americas / Department of Human Development / Organization of American States / 1889 F Street NW / Washington, DC 20006 / Tel: 202-458-6166 / scholarships@oas.org http://www.oas.org/EN/PINFO/HR/ gen_information.htm

Paul and Daisy Soros Fellowship for New Americans

Eligible	Immigrants working toward citizenship and new citizens
Eligible	All colleges and universities
Host Institution	Paul and Daisy Soros Foundation
App Deadline	Early November
Contact	The Paul and Daisy Soros Fellowship for New Americans / 400 West 59th Street / New York, NY 10019 / Tel: 212-547-6926 / Fax: 212-548-4623 http://www.pdsoros.org

Peace Corps Fellowships

Eligible	College graduates
Eligible	All colleges and universities
Host Institution	Peace Corps
App Deadline	Rolling basis
Contact	Peace Corps / Paul D. Coverdell Peace Corps Headquarters / 1111 20th Street NW / Washington, DC 20526 / Tel: 800-424-8580 http://www.peacecorps.gov/index.cfm?&

Programs in Biomedical Sciences Fellowships

Eligible	PhD students
Eligible	All colleges and universities
Host Institution	University of Michigan
App Deadline	Mid-December
Contact	Program In Biomedical Sciences / University of Michigan Medical School / 2960 Taubman Medical Library / 1150 W. Medical Center Drive, Box 0619 / Ann Arbor, MI 48109-0619 http://www.med.umich.edu/pibs/support.htm

Public Allies

Eligible	All students
Eligible	All colleges and universities
Host Institution	Public Allies
App Deadline	Varies by site
Contact	Public Allies, Inc. / 633 W. Wisconsin Ave., #610 / Milwaukee, WI 53203 / Tel: 414-273-0533 / Fax: 414-273-0543 / admin@publicallies.org www.publicallies.org

Public Policy and International Affairs Junior Summer Institute

Eligible	College juniors
Eligible	All colleges and universities
Host Institution	PPIA
App Deadline	Varies by institute
Contact	PPIA Program / 1029 Vermont Avenue NW, Suite 800 / Washington, DC 20005 / Tel: 202-496-0139 / Fax: 202-496-0134 http://www.ppiaprogram.org/programs/jsi.php

Rhodes Scholarship

Eligible	All students with outstanding academic performance
Eligible	All colleges and universities (applicants must be endorsed by their home institutions)
Host Institution	Oxford University
App Deadline	Early October
Contact	Elliot F. Gerson / 8229 Boone Boulevard, Suite 240 / Vienna, VA 22182/ amecs@rhodesscholar.org http://www.rhodesscholar.org/

Robert Bosch Foundation Fellowship Program

Eligible	Young American professionals (ages 23–34) who want to work and study in Germany
Eligible	All colleges and universities
Host Institution	CDS International
App Deadline	Mid-October
Contact	CDS International / 871 United Nations Plaza (First Avenue at 49th Street) / New York, NY 10017-1814 / Tel: 212-497-3500 / Fax: 212-497-3535 / info@cesintl.org http://www.cdsintl.org/fromusa/bosch.htm

Rotary International Ambassadorial Scholarships

Eligible	Undergraduates and graduates
Eligible	All colleges and universities
Host Institution	Rotary International
App Deadline	Varies by scholarship
Contact	Rotary International / One Rotary Center / 1560 Sherman Ave. / Evanston, IL 60201 / Tel: 847-866-3000 / Fax: 847-328-8554 or 847-328-8281 http://www.rotary.org/foundation/educational/amb_scho/

Rotary World Peace Fellowship

Eligible	Graduate students
Eligible	Rotary Centers for International Studies
Host Institution	Rotary International
App Deadline	Multiple deadlines apply to club, district, and world levels of Rotary administration
Contact	Rotary International / One Rotary Center / 1560 Sherman Ave. / Evanston, IL 60201 /

Tel: 847-866-3000 / Fax: 847-328-8554 or
847-328-8281
http://www.rotary.org/en/StudentsAndYouth/
EducationalPrograms/AmbassadorialScholarships/
Pages/ridefault.aspx

Rural Service Fellows

Eligible	All students interested in working with nonprofits in a rural area of upstate New York
Eligible	All colleges and universities
Host Institution	United Way of Tompkins County
App Deadline	Early April
Contact	United Way Rural Fellowship Program / United Way of Tompkins County / 313 N. Aurora Street / Ithaca, NY 14850 / Tel: 607-272-8286 / Fax: 607-272-2736 http://www.hostithaca.com/vista/

Samuel Huntington Public Service Award

Eligible	Graduating seniors interested in one year of funds to serve anywhere in the world
Eligible	All colleges and universities
Host Institution	National Grid
App Deadline	Mid-February
Contact	The Samuel Hunting Fund / Attn: Amy F. Stacy / 25 Research Drive / Westborough, MA 10582 / Tel: 508-389-3390 / amy-stacy@us.ngrid.com http://www.nationalgridus.com/commitment/ d4-1_award.asp

Science Education Programs

Eligible	Undergraduates, graduates, faculty
Eligible	All colleges and universities

Host Institution	Oak Ridge Institute for Science and Education
	DHS Scholarship and Fellowship Program
App Deadline	Varies by program
Contact	Wayne Stevenson / Director, Science Education
	Programs / Tel: 865-576-3424 /
	science.education@orau.org
	http://orise.orau.gov/sep/catalog.htm

Secretary Elaine L. Chao Internship Program

Eligible	All students
Eligible	All colleges and universities
Host Institution	U.S. Department of Labor
App Deadline	Mid-September for fall awards (see Web page)
Contact	U.S. Department of Labor / Frances Perkins
	Building / 200 Constitution Avenue NW /
	Washington, DC 20201 / Tel: 877-889-5627
	http://www.dol.gov/_sec/media/internprogram.htm

Segal AmeriCorps Education Award

Eligible	AmericCorps members who have completed their
	service with the organization
Eligible	All colleges and universities
Host Institution	AmeriCorps
App Deadline	Varies
Contact	AmeriCorps / 1201 New York Avenue NW /
	Washington, DC 20525 /Tel: 202-606-5000 /
	TTY: 202-606-3472 / questions@americorps.org
	http://www.americorps.org/default.asp

Smithsonian Institute Graduate Student Fellowship

Eligible	Graduate students
Eligible	All colleges and universities
Host Institution	Smithsonian Opportunities for Research and Study

App Deadline	Varies by program
Contact	Office of Research Training and Services / Smithsonian Institution / 470 L'Enfant Plaza SW, Suite 7102 / MRC 902 PO Box 37012 / Washington, DC 20013-7012 / Tel: 202-633-7070 / siofg@si.edu http://www.si.edu/ofg/fell.htm

Society for Technical Communication Scholarships

Eligible	All students
Eligible	All colleges, universities, and technical schools
Host Institution	Society for Technical Communication
App Deadline	Varies by scholarship
Contact	Society of Technical Communication / 901 N. Stuart Street, Suite 904 / Arlington, VA 22203-1822 / Tel: 703-522-4114 http://www.stc.org/edu/scholarshipInfo01.asp

Society of Women Engineers Scholarships

Eligible	Female undergraduate and graduate students
Eligible	All colleges and universities that have ABET-accredited engineering programs
Host Institution	The Society of Women Engineers
App Deadline	Varies by scholarship
Contact	Society of Women Engineers / 230 E. Ohio Street, Suite 400 / Chicago, IL 60611-3265 / Tel: 312-596-5223 http://www.swe.org

Student Inventors Scholarships

Eligible	All full-time students
Eligible	All colleges and universities
Host Institution	National Inventors Hall of Fame Foundation
App Deadline	Mid-June

Contact   Collegiate Inventors Competition / 221 S.
                      Broadway Street / Akron, OH 44308-1505 /
                      Tel: 330-849-6887 / collegiate@invent.org
                      http://www.invent.org/collegiate

Student Video Scholarships

Eligible   Full-time college students who can show visually
                      (in five minutes or less in video form) "One Person
                      Can Make A Difference"
Eligible   All colleges and universities
Host Institution   The Christophers
App Deadline   Early June
Contact   The Christophers / Tel: 212-759-4050 /
                      youth@christophers.org
                      http://www.christophers.org/vidcon2K.html

Supervalu Scholarships

Eligible   Supervalu associates that are in pharmacy school
Eligible   All pharmacy schools
Host Institution   Supervalu Pharmacies
App Deadline   See Web site for details
Contact   Adam Konrad, Pharmacist Recruiter /
                      SUPERVALU Pharmacies HT /
                      19011 Lake Drive East / Chanhassen, MN 55317 /
                      Tel: 952-294-7252 / Fax: 952-294-7190 /
                      adam.a.konrad@supervalu.com
                      http://www.supervalupharmacies.com/
                      students/scholarship_loans.asp#Scholarship

Teach for America

Eligible   Graduating seniors or recent college graduates
Eligible   All colleges and universities
Host Institution   Teach for America

App Deadline: Rolling·deadlines between September and the
                  following February
Contact   Teach for America / 315 West 36th Street, 7th
                  Floor / New York, NY 10018 /
                  Toll: 800-832-1230 / Tel: 212-279-2080 /
                  Fax: 212-279-2081 /
                  admissions@teachforamerica.org
                  http://www.teachforamerica.org

Teaching Assistant Program in France

Eligible   Prospective English teachers that are fluent in
                  French
Eligible   All colleges and universities
Host Institution French Embassy
App Deadline   See Web site for details
Contact   Assistant Program / A.C.A.C./ French Embassy /
                  4101 Reservoir Road / Washington, DC 20007 /
                  Tel: 202-944-6294 / Tax: 202-944-6268 /
                  assistant.washington-amba@diplomatie.gouv.fr
                  http://www.frenchculture.org/a_assistantship-
                  program_195.cfm

Technical Minority Scholarship Program

Eligible   Minority undergraduate and graduate students
Eligible   All colleges and universities
Host Institution Xerox
App Deadline   Late September
Contact   Xerox Technical Minority Scholarship Program /
                  150 State Street, 4th Floor / Rochester, NY 14614
                  http://www.xerox.com/go/xrx/template/
                  009.jsp?view=Feature&Xcntry=USA&Xlang=en_
                  US&ed_name=Careers_Technical_Scholarship

Think Swiss Research Fellowship

Eligible	Graduate students
Eligible	All colleges and universities
Host Institution	The Consulate of Switzerland in Boston, its sister office swissnex in Fan Francisco, and the Office of Science, Technology and Higher Education (OSTHE) at the Embassy of Switzerland in Washington, DC, are the leading houses of the program.
App Deadline	Late April
Contact	Office of Science, Technology and Higher Education (OSTHE) / Embassy of Switzerland / 2900 Cathedral Avenue NW / Washington, DC 20008 / Tel: 202-745-7958 / www.swissemb.org/scitech / http://www.thinkswiss.org/

Thomas J. Watson Fellowship Program

Eligible	Recent college graduates
Eligible	Limited to invited colleges and universities. See Web site for details
Host Institution	Thomas J. Watson Foundation
App Deadline	Early November
Contact	Thomas J. Watson Fellowship Program / 810 7th Avenue, 31st Floor / New York, NY 10019 / Tel: 212-245-8859 / Fax: 212-245-8860 / tiw@watsonfellowship.org http://watsonfellowship.org

Thomas R. Pickering Graduate and Undergraduate Foreign Affairs Fellowship

Eligible	Students planning to work for the U.S. Department of State in the Foreign Service and are sophomores with a cumulative GPA of 3.2 or higher

Eligible   All colleges and universities
Host Institution   The Woodrow Wilson National Fellowship
                    Foundation and the U.S. Department of State
App Deadline   Early February
Contact   Dr. Richard Hope / Director Foreign Affairs
                    Fellowship Program / The Woodrow Wilson
                    National Fellowship Foundation / PO Box 2437 /
                    Princeton, NJ 08543-2437 /
                    pickeringfaf@woodrow.org
                    http://www.woodrow.org/public-
                    policy/UFAFapplication.php

Tylenol Scholarship

Eligible   All students
Eligible   All colleges and universities
Host Institution   McNeil Consumer Healthcare, a Division of
                    McNeil PPC, Inc.
App Deadline   See Web page
Contact   Tel: 1-877-TYLENOL (English)
                    or 1-888-466-8746 (Spanish)
                    http://www.tylenol.com/
                    page.jhtml?id=tylenol/news/subptyschol.inc

United Negro College Fund Scholarships

Eligible   Varies by scholarship
Eligible   All colleges and universities
Host Institution   United Negro College Fund
App Deadline   Varies by scholarship
Contact   United Negro College Fund / 8260 Willow Oaks
                    Corporate Drive / PO Box 10444 / Fairfax,
                    VA 22031-8004 / Tel: 800-331-2244
                    http://www.uncf.org/forstudents/scholarship.asp

U.S. Department of State Student Internships

Eligible   All students
Eligible   All colleges and universities
Host Institution   U.S. Department of State
App Deadline   November 1 for summer internships, March 1 for
                      fall internships,
                      July for spring internships
Contact   U.S. Department of State / HR/REE/REC / 2401
                      E. Street NW, Suite 518 H / Washington,
                      DC 20522 / careers@state.gov
                      http://www.careers.state.gov/
                      students/programs.html#SIP

National Parks Internships (Cultural Resources Diversity Internship Program; Volunteers in the Parks)

Eligible   Varies by internship
Eligible   All colleges and universities
Host Institution   U.S. National Park Service
App Deadline   Varies by internship
Contact   National Capital Regional Office / National Park
                      Service / 1100 Ohio Drive SW / Washington,
                      DC 20242 / Tel: 202-619-7256
                      http://www.nps.gov/personnel/intern.htm

Wellstone Fellowship for Social Justice

Eligible   All minority undergraduate and graduate students
                      or recent graduates
Eligible   All colleges and universities
Host Institution   Families U.S.A.
App Deadline   Early February
Contact   Families U.S.A. / 1201 New York Avenue, Suite
                      1100 / Washington, DC 20005 /
                      Tel: 202-628-3030 / Fax: 202-347-2417 /
                      info@familiesusa.org

http://www.familiesusa.org/about/wellstone-fellowship-about.html

White House Fellows Program

Eligible	All students who have begun their careers
Eligible	All colleges and universities
Host Institution	The White House
App Deadline	Early February
Contact	White House Fellows Program / c/o O.P.M. - Sheila Coates / 1900 East Street NW, Room B431 / Washington, DC 20415 / Tel: 202-606-1818 http://www.whitehouse.gov/fellows/

William E. Simon Fellowship for the Noble Purpose

Eligible	College seniors interested in civic service
Eligible	All colleges and universities
Host Institution	Intercollegiate Studies Institute
App Deadline	Mid-February
Contact	Graduate Fellowships Program / Intercollegiate Studies Institute / 3901 Centerville Road / PO Box 4431 / Wilmington, DE 19807-0431 / Tel: 302-652-4600 / Fax: 302-652-1760 / awards@isi.org http://www.isi.org/programs/fellowships/simon.html

William Randolph Hearst Endowed Scholarship for Minority Students

Eligible	Minority undergraduate and graduate students who have excellent academic records and are in need financially
Eligible	All colleges and universities
Host Institution	The Aspen Institute
App Deadline	Mid-March

Contact   Erin Taber, Program Coordinator / The Aspen
                      Institute / One DuPont Circle, Suite 700 /
                      Washington, DC 20036
                      http://www.apsanet.org/content_11389.cfm

World Teach

Eligible   Recent college graduates
Eligible   All colleges and universities
Host Institution   World Teach
App Deadline   Varies by program
Contact   WorldTeach / c/o Center for International
                      Development / Harvard University / Box 122 / 79
                      John F. Kenney Street / Cambridge, MA 02138
                      / Tel: 1-800-4-TEACH-0 (483-2240) or 617-495-
                      5527 / Fax: 617-495-1599 / General Information:
                      info@worldteach.org / Applicant
                      Information: admissions@worldteach.org
                      http://www.worldteach.org

Index

academic affairs, fellowship office housing in, 62

achievement-based scholarship programs. *See* Coca-Cola Scholars Foundation; Fulbright program; NIH/Oxford/Cambridge Scholars Program

advisors. *See* scholarship advisors

Africa, exchange programs in, 3

African American students
Gilman Scholarship recipients, 5
I Have Risen: Essays by African American Youth, 23
Ron Brown Scholar Program, 23, 24–25

Allen, Danielle M.
current location, 32
scholar comment, 26

alumni
Coca-Cola Scholars Advisory Board, 25
mentoring programs, 71–72

ambassadorial role, of exchange scholars, 7

American University
Career Center, 56
Washington Semester Program, 58

application process
essays (*see* essays)
feedback process, 10
interviewing (*see* interviewing)
questions, responses to, 13–15
selection process (*see* selection process)
success, measurement of, 61–62
timeline, 29–30
for Truman Scholarship, 11–13

arts exchange program, 6

Asia, exchange programs in, 3

Assessing and Evaluating Honors Programs and Honors Colleges: A Practical Handbook to Innovations in Undergraduate Research and Honors Education, 97

At the Interface of Scholarship and Teaching: How to Develop and Administer Institutional Undergraduate Research Programs, 95–96

biomedical graduate education
National Institutes of Health partnerships, 35, 37–39
program characteristics, 35–37

biomedical research. *See* biomedical graduate education; biomedical undergraduate education

biomedical undergraduate education, NIH internships, 99

Bonner Leaders Program Campus, 56–57

Boyer Commission Report, 96

Bridgeman, Theresa
on application timelines, 29
current location, 32
scholar comment, 27–28

Brookings Institution Initiative on International Volunteering and Service, 57

Building Bridges Program, 57

Campus Compact, 52, 56

campus context, 62–63, 88

campus culture, 60–62, 88

candidate identification process, 30

capacity building, at campus level, 56–57

Career Center, American University, 56

career options, in scholarship advising, 62

Carter Center, Georgia, 58

change agent, versus facilitator, 16

Chokshi, Dave
on application timelines, 29
current location, 32
scholar comment, 26, 27

Churchill Scholars, NIH/Oxford/Cambridge
Scholarship extension for, 40
Coca-Cola Scholars Foundation
essay requirement, 22–23
scholar comments, 26, 27–28, 31
selection process, 25–26
collaborative leadership
masking effect on application, 14
of millennial generation, 16–17
College of William and Mary, student
recruitment practices, 63–64
communication skills, at interviews, 80
Community Research and Learning Network
(CoRAL), 54–55, 56
community service
by Coca-Cola Scholars, 28
Corporation for National and
Community Service, 57
Everett Public Service Internship, 57
in exchange programs, 6
by Mitchell Scholars, 24
value of, 28
computer programmers, role in selection
process, 46
Corella and Bertram F. Bonner Foundation,
56–57
Corporation for National and Community
Service, 57
Council on Undergraduate Research (CUR)
overview, 94–96
Posters on the Hill program, 101
Critical Language Scholarship Program, 4
CUR Dialogues, 95
CUR Quarterly, 95

Department of Education, International
Education Week, 6
Department of Energy, science
undergraduate laboratory internships,
99–100
Department of Health and Human Services.
See National Institutes of Health
Department of State
Academic Programs Office, 2 (*see also
individual programs*)
diversity programs, 4–5
exchange legislative mission, 3
Fulbright program (*see* Fulbright
program)
joint higher-education-government
delegations, 2

Open Doors study, 6
diversity
African American students (*see* African
American students)
Department of State programs, 4–5
of faculty (*see* faculty diversity)
Gilman Scholarship, 5, 7
Union College, 71–72
University of Illinois at Chicago,
72–73
University of Maryland at Baltimore
County, 68–69
University of Rochester, 69–71
doctoral education. *See* graduate education

educational exchange programs. *See also
individual programs*
community service, 6
exchange legislative mission, 3
joint higher-education-government
delegations, 2
undergraduate programs, 4–5, 6
essays
Coca-Cola Scholars Foundation
requirements, 22–23
editing of, 27, 30
leadership assessment, tool for, 12, 13–17
Ron Brown Scholar Program
requirements, 23
European Union
exchange programs, presence of, 3–4
Great Britain (*see* United Kingdom)
National Institutes of Health
partnerships in, 39
evaluation
*Assessing and Evaluating Honors Programs
and Honors Colleges: A Practical
Handbook to Innovations in
Undergraduate Research and Honors
Education*, 97
of experiential learning activities, 55
Evans, Vanessa
affiliation, 21
on Ron Brown scholars, 25
Everett Public Service Internship, 57
exchange programs. *See* educational exchange
programs
experiential education. *See also* internships;
service learning
online resources, 56–57
support for, 52–55

facilitator, versus change agent, 16
Faculty and Administrators Network sessions
   (NCUR), 100–101
faculty diversity
   University of Illinois at Chicago, 72–73
   University of Rochester, 70
faculty participation
   in application development, 64–65
   in experiential education programming,
     53–54
   facilitation of, 88, 89
   partnering models, 87
   in practice interviews, 78, 79–80
   recognition of, 91
   scholarship advisory boards, 90–92
   scholarship candidate identification, 63
   scholarship effort advancement, 86–87
federal funding
   Department of Education, 6
   Department of Energy, 99–100
   Department of State (*see* Department of
     State)
   for undergraduate research, 97–100
feedback, on applications, 10–11
fellowship advisors. *See* scholarship advisors
fellowship office, housing of, 62
fellowships, online resources, 57
foreign-language teaching program, 4
foreign student leaders, exchange programs
   for, 4, 6
Fulbright program
   ambassadorial role, 7
   language projects, 4
   legislative mission, 3
   MTVU pilot project, 5
   participant trends, 3–4
   scholar comments, 28–29
fusion arts exchange program, 6

Gates Cambridge Scholarship, interview
   questions, 77–78, 81
Gilman Scholarship
   ambassadorial role, 7
   overview, 5
Global Service Fellowships, 57
Gottesman, Michael, 34
Graduate education
   biomedical research (*see* biomedical
     graduate education)
   Carter Center assistantships, 58
   Graduate Partnerships Program (NIH), 34

MD/PhD training, 38–39, 40–41
   Three Magical Letters: Getting to PhD, 74
   time to graduate, 35–36
   in the United Kingdom, 37
   University of Illinois at Chicago
     fellowships, 73
Graduate Partnerships Program (NIH), 34
Great Britain. *See* United Kingdom
GRE scores, for NIH awards, 40

Henry, Antonia J.
   current location, 23, 32
   essay by, 23
Hispanic American students, with Gilman
   Scholarships, 5
honors education
   National Collegiate Honors Council, 97
   publications on, 97
   University of Arizona, 90
Honors in Practice, 97
Howard Hughes Medical Institutes/NIH
   Research Scholars Program, 40–41
Hughes, Karen, 2

identification process. *See* candidate
   identification process
*I Have Risen: Essays by African American
   Youth*, 23
information collection
   at College of William and Mary, 64
   selection process, role in, 46
   for underrepresented student
     recruitment, 73, 74
Institutional Nomination Letter, for Truman
   Scholarship, 12
international education. *See also individual
   programs*
   experiential learning opportunities, 57
   fusion arts exchange program, 6
   International Education Week, 6
   legislative mission, 3
   NIH/Oxford/Cambridge Scholars
     Program, 35, 37–39
   study abroad (*see* study abroad programs)
   Summit of U.S. College and University
     Presidents on International Education, 2
International Education Week, 6
intern programs
   Carter Center opportunities, 58
   Department of Energy opportunities,
     99–100

Everett Public Service Internship, 57
NIH Summer Intern Program, 39–41
online resources for, 58
in Washington, DC, 56, 57, 58
interviewing
application review as preparation, 77, 78
external factors, 82–83
Gates Cambridge Scholarship interview
questions, 77–78, 81
practice interviews, 76–77, 78–80
self-assessment of applicant, 81
Iran, Fulbright foreign-language teaching
program, 4

Jane Goodall Institute, 57
Johnson, Gordon, 80
*Journal of the National Collegiate Honors
Council*, 97

language programs, 4
leadership
articulation of, 15–17
collaborative, 16–17
responses, helpful, 14–15
responses, ineffective, 13–14
in Truman Scholarships, 10, 11–17
Learn and Serve America, 57
Lenardo, Michael, 38
letter of recommendation, for Truman
Scholarship, 12
Lutte, Mark
current location, 32
scholar comment, 28–29

Maine, Senator George J. Mitchell
Scholarship Research Institute
overview, 23–24
scholar comments, 28–29
Mallory, Mike, 21
Marshall Scholars, NIH/Oxford/Cambridge
Scholarship extension, 40
MCAT scores, for NIH awards, 40
McCray, Suzanne, 21
McMichael, Andrew, 35
MD/PhD training, 38–39, 40–41
Medical Scientist Training Program, 38–39,
41
medical training
NIH/Oxford/Cambridge Scholars
Program, 38–39, 41
test scores, for NIH awards, 40

mental approach, to interviewing, 80
mentoring programs
by alumni, 71–72
dual mentoring projects, 39
merit-based scholarship programs. *See* Coca-
Cola Scholars Foundation; Fulbright
program; NIH/Oxford/Cambridge
Scholars Program
minority students
data needs for recruitment, 73, 74
Union College, 71–72
University of Illinois at Chicago, 72–73
University of Maryland at Baltimore
County, 68–69
University of Rochester, 69–71
Mitchell Scholars. *See* Senator George J.
Mitchell Scholarship Research Institute
Muhlenberg College
campus culture, 60
student research, 61, 62
Music Television college network, Fulbright
pilot program, 5–6

9/11 events, effect on exchange programs, 3
National Aeronautics and Space
Administration, Undergraduate
Student Research Program, 97–98
National Association of Colleges and
Employers, 56
National Association of Fellowship Advisors
2007 Boot Camp, 60
advisor list, 30
new advisor support, 64
National Collegiate Honors Council, 97
National Conferences on Undergraduate
Research (NCUR), 100–101
National Institute of Standards and
Technology, Summer Undergraduate
Research Fellowship Programs, 99
National Institutes of Health
Graduate Partnerships Program, 34
Howard Hughes Medical Institutes
partnership, 40–41
Medical Scientist Training Program,
38–39, 41
NIH/Oxford/Cambridge Scholars
Program, 35, 37–39
Postbaccalaureate Intramural Research
Training Award program, 34–35, 40
student preparation, for awards, 39–41
Summer Intern Program, 39–41, 99

undergraduate intern program, 99
Undergraduate Scholarship Program,
98–99
Wellcome Trust partnership, 39
National Science Foundation, Research
Experiences for Undergraduates, 98
National Security Language Initiative, 4
National Society for Experiential Education,
56
need-based programs. *See* Gilman
Scholarship; Ron Brown Scholar
Program
Nepal, schooling project, 31
networks
for advisors, 64, 88–89
faculty, 64–65, 100–101
NCUR Faculty and Administrators
Network, 100–101
on-campus, 88–89
NIH. *See* National Institutes of Health
NIH/Oxford/Cambridge Scholars Program,
35, 37–39
GRE/MCAT scores, 40
Northeastern University, fusion arts
exchange, 6
NSF. *See* National Science Foundation

online resources
advisor list, on NAFA Web site, 30
for experiential education, 52, 55,
56–58
Reinvention Center, University of
Miami, 96
Open Doors study, 6

partnering models
with faculty, 87
National Institutes of Health models (*see*
National Institutes of Health)
public-private partnerships, at State
Department, 5–6
Peters, Sir Keith, 35
Pomona College, candidate identification,
63
Postbaccalaureate Intramural Research
Training Award program (NIH),
34–35, 40
professional development opportunities
Council on Undergraduate Research
avenues, 95
for faculty, 55, 100

National Association of Fellowship
Advisors conference, 60
for undergraduates, 95, 100–101
publications
*I Have Risen: Essays by African American
Youth*, 23
*Assessing and Evaluating Honors Programs
and Honors Colleges: A Practical
Handbook to Innovations in
Undergraduate Research and Honors
Education*, 97
*At the Interface of Scholarship and
Teaching: How to Develop and
Administer Institutional
Undergraduate Research Programs*,
95–96
CUR Dialogues, 95
CUR Quarterly, 95
Honors in Practice, 97
*Journal of the National Collegiate Honors
Council*, 97
*Reinventing Undergraduate Education: A
Blueprint for America's Research
Universities*, 96
Three Magical Letters: Getting to PhD,
74
public-private partnerships, at State
Department, 5–6

questions
at Gates Cambridge Scholarship
interviews, 77–78, 81
generic types, 79
for self-assessment of applicant, 81
on Truman application, 12, 16
written responses, quality of, 13–15
Quint, Colleen
affiliation, 21
on Mitchell Scholars, 24

recruitment. *See* student recruitment
*Reinventing Undergraduate Education: A
Blueprint for America's Research
Universities*, 96
Reinvention Center, 96
reporting structure, 88
Research Experiences for Undergraduates
(NSF), 98
Rhodes Scholars, NIH/Oxford/Cambridge
Scholarship extension, 40
Rice, Condoleezza, 2

Ron Brown Scholar Program
  applicant essay, 23
  overview, 24–25
  scholar comments, 26–27
Roots and Shoots, 57

scholar comments
  Coca-Cola Scholars Foundation, 26,
    27–28, 31
  Ron Brown Scholar Program, 26–27
  Senator George J. Mitchell Scholarship
    program, 27–28
scholarship advising
  campus context, relevance of, 62–63, 88
  campus culture, role of, 60–62, 88
  promotional material, 64
  publications (*see* publications)
  in student recruitment, 63–64
  support networks in, 64–65, 88–89
scholarship advisors
  career options, 62
  higher education background of, 89
  NAFA support, 64
  role of, 45–46
  student perspectives of, 27, 28–29, 30
scholarship advisory boards, 90–92
scholarship preparation courses, 65
science education
  biomedical research (*see* biomedical
    graduate education; biomedical
    undergraduate education)
  Department of Energy, undergraduate
    laboratory internships, 99–100
selection process. *See also* application process
  applicant quality, 47
  interviewing (*see* interviewing)
  subjectivity of, 46–47
  transparency of, 47–48
self-assessment, of applicant, 81
Senator George J. Mitchell Scholarship
    Research Institute
  overview, 23–24
  scholar comments, 28–29
service learning, resource availability, 53
Sheppard, Stephen, 77
Srinivasan, Rajiv
  current location, 32
  scholar comment, 22
State Department. *See* Department of State
statisticians, role in selection process, 46
Stearns, Chris, 29

student affairs, fellowship office housing in,
    62
student recruitment
  College of William and Mary, 63–64
  of underrepresented populations (*see*
    underrepresented students)
study abroad programs
  Gilman Scholarship, 5, 7
  student experiences, 31
Sullivan, Lee
  current location, 32
  scholar comment, 31
summer programs
  Everett Public Service Internship, 57
  at Muhlenberg College, 61
  National Institute of Standards and
    Technology, Summer Undergraduate
    Research Fellowship Programs, 99
  National Institutes of Health Summer
    Intern Program, 39–41, 99–100
Summit of U.S. College and University
    Presidents on International
    Education, 2
syllabi
  for experiential learning activities,
    52, 56
  scholarship preparation courses, 65

Three Magical Letters: Getting to PhD, 74
Truman Foundation
  feedback process, 10
  review of comments, 10–11
Truman Scholarship, 10, 11–17
  application process, 11–13
  interview questions, 81

undergraduate exchange programs
  diversity programs, 4–5, 6
  for foreign student leaders, 4, 6
undergraduate research programs
  *Assessing and Evaluating Honors Programs
    and Honors Colleges: A Practical
    Handbook to Innovations in
    Undergraduate Research and Honors
    Education*, 97
  *At the Interface of Scholarship and
    Teaching: How to Develop and
    Administer Institutional
    Undergraduate Research Programs*,
    95–96
  biomedical education, 99

conference presentation opportunities, 100–101

Council on Undergraduate Research, 94–96

Department of Energy, science undergraduate laboratory internships, 99–100

National Aeronautics and Space Administration program, 97–98

National Collegiate Honors Council, 97

National Institute of Standards and Technology programs, 99

National Institutes of Health programs, 98–99

National Science Foundation program, 98

Reinventing Undergraduate Education: A Blueprint for America's Research Universities, 96

Reinvention Center, University of Miami, 96

summer programs, 39–41, 99–100

underrepresented students

data needs, for recruitment, 73, 74

Union College, 71–72

University of Illinois at Chicago, 72–73

University of Maryland at Baltimore County, 68–69

University of Rochester, 69–71

Union College, 71–72

United Kingdom

graduate training style, 37

NIH partnerships, 35, 37–39

University of Arizona, scholarship advisory board, 90–92

University of Arkansas, Office of Nationally Competitive Awards, 76

University of Cambridge, NIH partnerships, 35, 37–39

University of Illinois at Chicago, 72–73

University of Maryland at Baltimore County, 68–69

University of Miami, Reinvention Center, 96

University of Nebraska-Lincoln, Undergraduate Creative Activities and Research Experiences Program, 101

University of Oxford, NIH partnerships, 35, 37–39

University of Rochester, 69–71

urban universities, student recruitment at, 72–73

Varmus, Harold, 34

volunteer service

community service (*see* community service)

international programs, 6, 57

Washington Center for Internships and Academic Seminars, 58

Washington, DC

Community Research and Learning Network (CoRAL), 54–55, 56

experiential learning opportunities, 57, 58

Washington Semester Program, American University, 58

Web sites. *See also* online resources

experiential education, promotion of, 55

Wellcome Trust, 39

Williams, A. Damian

current location, 32

scholar comment, 27